REIKI

Heal Yourself & Others with Reiki. Clear Negative
Energy & Start Manifesting Positive Outcomes
Through the Ancient Healing Power of Reiki.

Subscribe To Sofia Visconti

As a subscriber you will receive a Free Gift + You wil be
the first to hear about new books, articles and more
exclusives just for you

Click Here

CONTENTS

INTRODUCTION

The energy of the universe is vast and omnipresent, affecting the world as we know it. Reiki encompasses this energy, using it to heal and restore inner balance. Aren't you eager to find out how to be in sync with the world around you? Reach deep within your soul and discover a new perspective in life, away from toxic thoughts that have been poisoning your mind. Have faith in the universe, as it has been here since the beginning of time. Feel the energy flowing through you and try to understand it.

I know this might seem too vague, filling you with more questions than you had before. Trust me, my goal is not to confuse you. On the contrary, this book is not going to be overly complicated, but it will enlighten you. What you are looking for is a clear, helpful guide to Reiki, and that is exactly what you are going to get. Chapter by chapter, I will show you how to use the energy of the universe to heal yourself, as well as others.

This is a wonderful spiritual journey you are setting out to experience, that will reveal things about your own existence that you may never have considered in the past. Don't be afraid of letting go of the things that have been dragging you down, but instead trust in the powerful universal energy to heal you. Dive into the mysteries of life and explore yourself as you go. This will be an exciting time, for sure!

Obviously, there are many people who have a distorted, incorrect opinion as to what Reiki really is. It is not always their fault, since there are so many different explanations that end up confusing people, instead of clearing the air for them. Half-truths are often more dangerous than actual, straight-up lies. People who tend to have an opinion about everything in life appear to hold the secrets to universal knowledge. Ironically, these are the people who spread the worst misconceptions about things they know nothing about.

By bridging science and spirituality in an easy-to-comprehend way, I will try to shed light on what Reiki is all about and its benefits. Away from conflicting information and biased opinions, you will be able to discover the ancient healing powers of Reiki. These powers are bound to change your life forever. In a world constantly becoming more hectic and chaotic every single day, it is important to appreciate what truly matters.

About Me

I am Sofia Visconti, and I am very happy to introduce myself to you. Throughout my life, I have always found great inspiration in the world of spirituality. Drawn by the powers around us, I have dedicated my life toward studying the universe, learning its secrets, and passing on my knowledge to others. I am an Amazon best-selling author with a variety of books on healing, spirituality, and everything in between. Different cultures fascinate me, so I delve into their mysteries to discover new worlds of spiritual and other types of wisdom. Through careful observation and a lot of study, I have opened up the door to a new perspective that I apply to my life every day.

There have been times when I found myself wondering about my place in the world. I did not know if there was any meaning or if my existence was purely random. Such questions flooded my mind, keeping me up at night. Is there a deeper connection between humans and the universe? Is there a fabric keeping us all in balance? Or maybe everything can be attributed to chance?

Nowadays, a lot has changed. I no longer feel insecure, nor do I have as many questions as I once did. Obviously, life is a never-ending lesson for us all. We keep learning as we go, through a "trial and error" strategy. Each experience holds a separate gift to offer us, and it is in our hands to make the most of it. I was blessed to have acquired invaluable wisdom through my journeys, so as to see more clearly what lies ahead.

In this book, I have focused on Reiki and its overwhelming power. Its roots date back to ancient times, having survived through centuries. Reiki is a living, breathing concept, encompassing the philosophies of East Asia in a holistic approach that mends, soothes, and balances. My experience has taught me to respect the past, always in pursuit of adjusting it to contemporary needs.

Without Reiki teachings, I would probably be a lot different to the person I am today. Through Reiki, I have learned how to appreciate the moment and be present, for myself and others. I do not poison my days, worrying about things that are way out of my hands. Instead, I focus on every single day. What I do is to make it count. Since I am grateful for all the blessings of my life, I keep smiling. This worldview has definitely changed me, improving my quality of life immensely.

I welcome you to my book with open arms. Rather than offering just another Reiki tutorial, I aim at providing a hands-on, practical option for you to read and learn from. My goal is to educate you on the background of this Asian philosophy, but without boring you with details or overly complicating things. As you read through the chapters, I hope your determination to follow this spiritual path becomes stronger. From my personal point of view, I am sure this is going to happen...Enjoy and stay blessed!

A New Spiritual Adventure: Are You Ready?

New beginnings are always exciting, as they are filled with so many fabulous opportunities. However, not everyone is ready for a change. There are people who have become so accustomed to their current situation that they find it hard to let go. In this case, any hope of ever changing something in your life seems to crumble into pieces. On the other hand, there are those who continuously crave the change. They do whatever it takes to experiment with different things and are always on edge.

None of these two very distinct categories qualifies as a great candidate for Reiki practice. If you are truly determined to improve your life, then you need to commit to that for the long run. You cannot base your decision on an impulse, nor can you set out on this spiritual adventure purely for the sake of starting fresh. Either way, your experience is going to be short lived. So, it would be prudent on your end to think twice before you dip your feet into the water.

Doing research always helps out, shedding light on things that will come to the surface, one way or another. Unless you have abundant time to waste, you need to be confident about your decision beforehand. This is why you should ask yourself if you are willing to do whatever it takes, in order to enjoy a healthier, happier life from now on; to some, this question is purely rhetorical and requires no answer. However, there are people who feel overwhelmed by their life as it is and do not have the time, or willpower, for anything radical.

As long as you are fully aware of the challenge ahead, you need to shield yourself. Set realistic goals, so as not to get discouraged along the way. There is no point in anticipating getting to the highest level of attunement after just a few weeks of Reiki sessions. The same applies if you practice incorrectly. It makes perfect sense that everyone has a different pace of progress. This is absolutely fine. No one is going to criticize you for taking the time and easing yourself into this journey.

Nevertheless, you cannot expect to become an expert overnight. If you are looking for a quick fix, Reiki is not the place for you. Unlike what some people might think, it is not just a trend. It will not fade away after a while. Reiki has been known to man since antiquity, and it encompasses a concept that has been known since the beginning of time. The universal force of energy is something you find in various cultures of the world. Having said that, it takes much more than an occasional session to indulge in Reiki and to fully comprehend its essence. You need to devote time and effort if you want to succeed in your endeavor.

Ultimately, what you need to consider is whether you believe that you can do it. You have the colors, and you have the canvas before you. Now it is time to paint. Use your imagination and gather inspiration from anything that fascinates you in life. Do not be afraid to fail; after all, failure is the pillar of success—you cannot have the one without the other. As soon as you realize that your future is in your hands, you are ready to create the life that you want.

If you have connected all the dots so far, now it is time to jump right in. Discover Reiki from its past roots, all the way up to the present. Feel free to explore its multiple aspects, finding the exact concept that ticks all the boxes for you. Do not let others define you and dictate what you do in your life; instead, clear out all negative thoughts, and restore your spiritual balance. Find your mental clarity, and heal yourself, as well as others through Reiki. A magnificent journey has just begun—welcome on board!

CHAPTER 1
WHAT IS REIKI?

Reiki is an alternative form of treatment to Western medicine. It became popular in the 1800s in Japan, and soon after it started spreading to the rest of the world. Using the energy of the universe, Reiki practitioners are able to heal the body from pain. The name Reiki derives from "Rei," which means "the wisdom of God," and "Ki," which means "the power of energy in life." If you believe there is inexhaustible power within your body, waiting to be awakened, then you are definitely on the right track.

Reiki is a divine gift, which has been handed over to mankind from above. A higher power has contributed to passing on that invaluable knowledge to people. The main reason behind this divine sharing has been to assist humans in their spiritual evolution. Knowledge is a powerful tool. The precious knowledge relevant to Reiki has made people turn to their roots, in pursuit of the connecting glue that has always kept them in balance with the universe. What if there is a power connecting us all?

From what Reiki teaches us, there are various energy fields all over the body. Depending on the root of each condition, different energy fields are targeted. Energy is transferred through the palms of the practitioner to specific parts of the body. This energy is powerful, and you can feel it concentrating. This is why you feel a welcoming sense of warmth throughout the Reiki session. It comforts you, allowing you to relax and restore your lost balance from within. The basic principle of passing on the energy from the palm to the body is called the attunement process.

Man is considered a complex entity, with multiple different layers. There are the physical, as well as the emotional, mental, and spiritual levels, all of which define humans. Even more impressive is the existence of a virtual blanket of light, covering the physical body. This layer is called an aura and represents a powerful field of energy. As you can see, Reiki penetrates the various layers of the body, in pursuit of balancing every single aspect of existence. For an individual to feel complete, all these levels must be in harmony. Otherwise, the balance is disrupted, and the repercussions are soon to appear.

There are many people still in disbelief when it comes to Reiki. They feel like they are not getting enough tangible evidence. However, universal life force is indisputable. It is everywhere around us. Energy stagnates in several parts of the body, in cases of injury or illness. Therefore, the patient needs to unblock the energy and release it. Despite the fact that you cannot see it, you can still feel it. Actually, patients do feel the benefits of the energy flowing through them. They understand the difference in their body. It is remarkable how much better they feel, without having resorted to any medication.

This raw form of energy comes from the universe and is directed within your body. Can you grasp the concept? The universe ensures that you are fueled with the power you need, so as to thrive in life. You are deeply and indisputably connected to the world. You are a part of the universe, in absolute harmony with your surroundings. Even if you feel out of sync, you still hold the missing link. You can find your inner balance once more, by restoring the energy flow through your chakras. These are the energy centers located throughout your body, allowing the smoothest transition, inside and out, of energy.

Some people argue about the validity of Reiki because there are not many scientific studies to back up its claims. There is nothing wrong in conducting scientific studies, obviously. But there are things that cannot be measured like that. Reiki makes patients feel better. This is a given. It has been shown again and again. Patients turn to this holistic treatment, alongside other healing options that are not backed up by science. Why would they do it, unless they felt that they received some sort of benefit out of the entire process? Most people find peace of mind and get instant relief of their pain. They report it in studies, get answers to their questions, and want to spread the word of Reiki.

However, mending the soul and tuning your inner balance clock are not things that you can see. You cannot measure the energy flow prior to the Reiki session and right after having completed a course. This means that statistics will not be able to reveal the value of Reiki in its fullness. Something will always be found lacking, which is of course perfectly understandable. Reiki is not a pill that you take as a remedy to fight off your viral infection. It does not work like that. The blessings that you receive through your Reiki sessions are abundant, but they are fluid. They are not fixed for every single person.

The energy flow affects patients differently. Depending on their overall health state and their personalized demands, Reiki improves their life in multiple layers. It enables them to suffer less and hope more. Not many prescribed medicines can boast about having the same effects on patients, can they? More than that, almost all medications come with a wide list of side effects. So, you might aim at curing a specific condition and end up needing medicines for its side effects. If you add that to the overconsumption of pills and the hospitalization that seems to skyrocket year by year, you can see that the current situation calls for a change.

Reiki is all about the spirit and its alignment with the body and soul. Most illnesses stem from an imbalance between these different aspects in life. As the flow of energy is improved, the results are amazing. The patient feels much better, and this has an impact not only on the symptoms of the disease. There are great benefits related to overall wellness. Patients report feeling invigorated, filled with energy, and ready to tackle life's challenges. Even if this is a mild, noninvasive treatment originating from the depths of East Asia, it has managed to win its place in every part of the world.

Body, mind, and spirit. This is what Reiki focuses on healing. When something is off, you cannot expect others to be in harmony. Hence, you should not limit your therapeutic approach to just one of these core concepts. Instead, you ought to target them all, and make sure everything is in sync. Reiki ensures there is a steady energy flow throughout the body, allowing the mind to be at ease. The spirit is free to relax and wander the paths of the unknown—the perfect balance, inside and out!

The History of Reiki

Universal life force has been around since the very beginning of time. However, as pointed out above, its current form is much more recent than that. Starting out in the 1800s in Japan, Reiki manifested a new perspective of a timeless concept. Some wise men started documenting its principles, as well as the philosophy, on which it was created. Nevertheless, the great boost in Reiki's popularity came with Mikao Usui. He is considered the father of Reiki, placing it in the modern frame we all know.

Born in 1865 in a small Japanese village, Mikao Usui was a young man of prominent ancestors and impressive educational background. He learned all about meditation, deep breathing techniques, and Tai Chi from a very young age. Then, he continued his training in spiritual healing, with focus on Buddhism, Zen, and Taoism philosophies. Upon covering all the fundamental principles about life, Mikao went on with his professional ventures for a while. He traveled a lot and met some truly inspirational people along the way.

Even though he worked in various professions over time, it was pure chance that led him to spirituality once more. After experimenting with a Zen retreat for several years, he decided to take a leap of faith. So, he set out on a unique journey to find himself, his true self. He climbed Mount Kurama, staying there for a period of 21 days, where he fasted and dove into the mysteries of meditation. This was an earth-shattering experience for Mikao Usui, later on known as Usui Sensei.

As the days went by, he felt differently. Even if at first, he doubted himself, he felt empowered. Before heading back to his normal daily routine, he experienced something spectacular. An overpowering energy went through him, entering from his head and flooding him with light. He decided to name that light "Reiki." After that, he felt completely rejuvenated. Even though he had spent so much time without food, he maintained his strength. It was something deeper than nourishment that drove him to continue on his path. He was so powerful that he performed four miracles, helping others without jeopardizing his own well-being.

This period on Mount Kurama has been eye opening for Mikao Usui. It was the first time he felt sure of his purpose. He went on to launch Usui Reiki Ryoho Gakkai, to teach this healing method to others. It was his conviction that the more people knew about Reiki, the better life would be for everyone. Unfortunately, during an earthquake in 1923, Usui and his students were forced to heal too many people left injured by nature's raw brutality. Even then, they coped with the challenges, rising up to the expectations.

Before his passing in 1926, Mikao Usui had managed to teach Reiki to over 2,000 people, and 20 Reiki masters. They were the ones responsible for passing on his knowledge and continuing his legacy. Among them were Chujiro Hayashi and Hawayo Takata. Hayashi had a medical background, and he devoted his life in Tokyo toward healing others. He optimized several positions and documented everything for the younger generations. By his passing, he had managed to make Reiki known to a whole new audience. This is why he is still remembered as one of the founders of Reiki.

Takata, on the other hand, was a patient from Tokyo who was having a rough time. She was about to undergo surgery but instead decided to receive Reiki treatment. Imagine how controversial such a decision would have been back then. Her illness disappeared, motivating her to spread the word of Reiki in the United States, and more particularly in Hawaii, where she lived. By the time of her death, she had already passed on her knowledge to 22 Reiki masters (The History of Usui Reiki and the Reiki Principles, n.d.).

Reiki has become more popular than ever before. This boils down to its deep roots and undeniable truth. As part of a holistic philosophy, it allows people to change their point of view. Although nowadays society is based on speed, Reiki introduces you to the deeper meaning of life. Treatment cannot happen overnight. People ought to look back to their past and realize what matters. Time should be cherished, health should be celebrated, and proper balance is key to a healthy lifestyle. With an impressive history and with a bright future ahead, Reiki is here to stay.

Debunking the Most Popular Myths of Reiki

There are several myths about Reiki, putting many people off actually comprehending its essence. One of the most frequent concerns is that Reiki is a form of religion. This could not be further from the truth. It is not a religion, nor could it be. I mentioned earlier the educational background of Mikao Usui, founder of Reiki as we know it today. He received his training on different philosophies, including the religious forms of Buddhism and Taoism. However, this does not mean Reiki promotes religion in any way. It is a spiritual journey that takes place, but without faith as a prerequisite.

People who practice Reiki do not automatically qualify as religious. On the contrary, they might not be pious at all. Belief is a personal matter, which does not affect your ability to practice Reiki. You can choose to be religious or instead reject religion. That being said, you need to believe in the universal energy of life. Otherwise, how can you use energy to heal yourself, as much as others? It is quite contradictory, if you think about it. Reiki teachings include faith in the divine force of the universe. However, they do not call for any type of religion.

Some people are worried about taking sides between Reiki and medicine. Another paradox, as many hospitals around the world have already introduced Reiki as an option worth exploring further. It goes without saying that Reiki does not condemn Western medicine altogether. There are many diseases requiring medication, surgery, physiotherapy, and so on. Nevertheless, Reiki can be used independently, or as a way to reduce chemicals and artificial substances poisoning our body.

It is true that people tend to consume medicines, even when they do not actually need them. Even the mildest headache or discomfort leads to a pill or maybe more. If you add to that all the supplements and vitamins available over the counter, you can see why it is so alarming. People did not always have such unobstructed access to medication. Obviously, this is a mixed blessing. In cases when there is a necessity to heal through medication, it is wonderful to have that option. However, in many cases medications are absolutely redundant. Unblocking the energy that has remained stagnant can work wonders for your body, mind, and soul instead. A win-win situation.

Moving forward with the false beliefs regarding Reiki, many consider it a type of massage. Under no circumstances should it be mistaken for a massage. The whole concept of Reiki is founded on the energy flow, which is accomplished through the palms. There is no actual touching. The Reiki practitioner gathers the energy on the palm, prior to releasing it to the patient. A similarity between Reiki and massage sessions is the feeling of tremendous relaxation afterward. However, the methodology is pretty different.

I do not know if you are familiar with astral projection. It is based on the realization that you can have an out-of-your-body experience, traveling through the different dimensions. Another concept to keep in mind is the lucid dream. In this case, you are dreaming. However, your mind is conscious of the fact that you are dreaming. I am fascinated by both these experiences, but I truly have to clarify that Reiki does not enhance any of those concepts. Reiki is concentrated on the energy flow, allowing your entity to achieve absolute balance with the universe. Astral projection is a very demanding path to walk on, where you consciously leave your body, and you wander off in search of intriguing stimuli. Unless you are 100% confident that you can handle astral projection, you are strongly advised to avoid it, as you will need to find your way back to your body again. For those of you worrying that Reiki holds a similar amount of risk, there really is nothing to keep you up at night.

Another widespread belief about Reiki is that it is nothing more than a placebo. A placebo is any medication holding no actual therapeutic value to the patient. Scientists sometimes give their patients placebos without them knowing, so as to study the effects vs. the actual medicine on trial (Wikipedia Contributors, 2019). One of the most important benefits deriving from a placebo is undoubtedly feeling better. Patients get a sense of reassurance from sticking to a remedy, even if this remedy is not real. On the contrary, Reiki is based on the real energy of the world. It is there for you to feel, even though you can't actually see that.

Reiki is not the answer to everything. It is a powerful tool in the hands of a conscious human being, who wants to find balance in life. But taking up Reiki does not mean that you have immediately resolved all your problems. Besides, it is not a quick fix. It is based on a philosophy that has survived through the centuries and is now as evergreen as ever. You must dedicate time and effort to read all about it. If you expect to take a magic pill, then you are definitely on the wrong path. Reiki is the timeless, universal energy force that runs through everything, dominating nature and dictating the balance of the world. Does that sound like a quick fix?

The following myth is very common, as it tends to affect even those who already practice Reiki. As you can imagine, it is quite tricky. More specifically, there are people who believe that Reiki is just one method. There is no room for alterations. However, this is not the way Reiki has been created. On the contrary, there are various different pathways to follow. Some Reiki healers claim that there are many more than seven chakras in the human body. Which option is correct? Well, things are not just black and white. Chakras are not physically present in the body. So, it is not like determining the exact location of your heart or lungs. In other words, there are many interpretations of Reiki, and they are all valid.

Is it just me, or do more people nowadays ask about Reiki? The more people search about it, the more the truth gets buried beneath the lies. One of the most frequent misconceptions I have been asked to comment on is that of correlating Reiki with martial arts. Well, the truth is that martial arts have always boasted increased popularity in the Western world. Apart from the archetypes of ancient times, martial arts encompass the principles of balancing your body, along with your soul. There is a deep sense of discipline, power stemming from within, and awareness when practicing martial arts.

Nonetheless, Reiki is much more than that. When you practice Reiki, you do not optimize your defensive moves. You will not become an excellent warrior, or at least not in its traditional sense. Reiki focuses on your spiritual journey toward healing. This bears no resemblance to martial arts. Of course, those who are fascinated by the philosophy of East Asia will definitely find both concepts appealing. So, it is safe to assume that the targeted audiences of both Reiki and martial arts coincide.

CHAPTER 2
REIKI ENERGY CLEARING

Energy flows within us. It is the very fabric of the world as we know it, allowing us to live in harmony with the rest of the universe. Life would not be the same without energy. There is a perfect balance in nature, ensuring that everything is in sync. The leaves on the trees, the gentle breeze, the sun with its silvery rays, the crystalline waters surrounding the land. It feels like a talented painter has painted the most wonderful canvas, depicting the world with the brightest colors. This is a genuine masterpiece, and it has all sprung from life force energy.

In this masterpiece of nature, it is crucial to go with the flow. The eternal balance of the world should not be disturbed or jeopardized in any way. Too much is at stake. You as a person ought to be in perfect alignment with this balance. The world expands through you, so you live and breathe in harmony with your surroundings. You have joined an endless dance, which instills life in every single being. Will you live up to the challenge, maintaining the rhythm and passing it on to others?

Every waking moment, energy flows through you. It floods you with light, giving you the strength to flourish and thrive in the world. Energy runs through your veins, spreading all over your body. It passes through you, from head to toes, surprising your every cell with an invigorating sensation. Have you ever felt a pleasant tingling, lifting your spirit? It is your energy in action. Once you learn how to tame this energy, nothing can stand in your way. You will broaden your horizons, opening up to innumerable opportunities.

Nonetheless, coming to terms with the very essence of life force energy can be hard. Not everyone knows how to handle it, ending up doing more harm than good. There are many obstacles, glitches, or more severe blockages threatening your well-being. Unless you master how to work around these obstacles and unblock your body, your mind, and your soul, you cannot anticipate experiencing energy's full blessing. You will constantly be tormented by "what ifs" and lost moments in time.

It is even more disturbing to know that you are the one to blame for these hindrances. Perhaps it is your defensive mechanism that has led you to block your energy flow. Maybe you have not dealt with a trauma from the past in a way that puts your mind at ease. We all have skeletons in our closet, after all. These issues of the past should be handled, though. Otherwise, they will creep in when we least expect it, haunting us forever. If you are interested in personal growth and if you want to overcome the barriers you have set for yourself, you need to unblock your energy.

Below, I am going to show you exactly how to do so, unraveling the mysteries of energy blockage. Why does this happen? How can you reverse the situation, allowing energy to flow abundantly through you? Turn your weakness into your most precious strength, skyrocketing your potential.

Use Reiki to Remove Obstacles and Blockages

It is essential that you use Reiki to rectify your energy blockage. This is only keeping you down, away from what you can actually achieve in life. You were meant for greatness, reaching your true self through a release of immense energy. In order to do that, you need to get rid of anything that has been holding you down. What makes you hesitant in life? What brings you sadness, depression, anxiety, or pain? All these elements should vanish into thin air, making way for happiness, bliss, and joy. You deserve that, don't you?

Sometimes, we get overwhelmed by traumatic memories.

These memories soon become bricks, building an enormous wall we can no longer penetrate. The wall keeps getting bigger and bigger. In contrast, we tend to feel smaller and smaller. How can we transform this feeling of inadequacy into our strength? It takes time, and effort to achieve that. We must work on our mentality, trying to figure out the root cause of this pile of negative past thoughts.

The truth lies within us. We know what reality holds, even though we do not admit that. But over time, this lack of honesty toward ourselves is only making us feel worse. We need to relax, taking a deep breath and appreciating the moment. This is easier said than done, obviously. You cannot always expect to act independently. It is crucial that you receive all the help you can get. And what a better way to discover your inner strength, than through Reiki?

As a noninvasive treatment targeting your body, mind, and soul, Reiki will enable you to unlock your energy. It will promote healing in a mild way, without pushing your body to its limits. Your body might accumulate negative energy subconsciously, and you do not even realize it. Violence is not the answer. You should not aim at extreme interventions because they may lead to an even greater shock for your body. Instead, gentle changes can be subtle, yet far more effective.

Reiki will help awaken your energy centers, channeling your energy in a balanced manner. Depending on the body parts that feel stressed, the Reiki practitioner will guide the energy to restore its perfectly balanced flow. As a result, you will feel a huge burden lifted off these body parts. Where there was discomfort, now will be lightness. Where there was pain, now will be pleasure. Reiki will accomplish that through absolute peace, with a hands-on healing technique that soothes the senses.

There are many different reasons for energy blocks. You might have injured yourself, concentrating the heat on specific parts of the body. Such traumas can be really bad for you, as they promote an aching feeling of agony. It is impossible to relax and experience life as it should be. On the contrary, you struggle to breathe. When you are in pain, it is not easy to distract yourself. You cannot experience anything other than the pain itself, which gets excruciating over time.

The same happens when you suffer from a psychological issue. Anxiety, disorders of all sorts, depression, panic attacks, and phobias are just a few of the mental health problems that pose a threat to your well-being. Such problems prevent you from enjoying life. This is where Reiki steps in, clearing the atmosphere and boosting your inner strength. It makes you recover, recharge, and start new. Even if the issues remain, your attitude toward them has changed.

One of the greatest sources of energy blockage, though, comes directly from us. We are the ones responsible, through our very own behavioral patterns. Have you ever found yourself admitting doing something harmful, yet not having the strength to stop? Even if you realize a particular fixation might be causing you trouble, you have no alternative. You keep on the same track, knowing that this damages your spirit. It crashes your dreams, withers your hopes, and prevents you from feeling good about yourself. Is it really how you want to live your life?

Reiki offers you a way out. It allows you to clear out your life from what makes you feel sad. You deserve to enjoy every moment. So, if a habit of yours holds you back, it is high time you unloaded that burden. Feel the negative energy leaving your body and welcome the wonderful energy that lights up your life instead. You will soon reap the benefits of this holistic spiritual experience and appreciate the moment. Although at the beginning, even the thought of changing your life will seem impossible, day by day with the help of Reiki you will notice a remarkable improvement that keeps getting better.

What It Feels Like

Some people might feel threatened by the unknown of jumping into deep dark waters, without knowing what lies on the seabed. If you fall into that category, then I am sure control plays an important role in your life. Therefore, it is very hard to trust others. In a similar pattern, it is difficult to let go of your worries and put your faith in another human being. However, you need to overcome your hesitation. When you do, things will get better.

Reiki offers you a subtle experience in restoring your energy flow from within. You must be utterly relaxed, so as to enable this experience to take place. Otherwise, you will not get the much anticipated results from your Reiki session. So, before scheduling your session, be sure to have a positive attitude, and be open to what is about to happen. Believe me, you will be thankful for having the opportunity to do that.

As soon as you start the session, you will immediately feel calm. That sense of absolute peace is so refreshing. Other than that, there are slight differences as to what each person experiences during Reiki sessions. Some people feel a pleasant tingling sensation throughout their body, while others feel cold or hot. Obviously, if you touch the hands of the Reiki practitioner, you will definitely feel their warmth. This is a welcoming surprise, the most eloquent proof that Reiki does work.

The more you relax, the more intense your experience is going to be. There is no doubt you should leave all your worries behind, concentrate on the energy flow, and relish the session. Do not hold your feelings inside, since they will block your energy and sabotage your progress. Once you release the tension, the stress, and the anxiety, you will soon notice a huge relief. Even if your condition requires a lot more sessions, this feeling of a weight lifted off your shoulders will still be enough to keep you motivated.

It is important to understand that you must always feel comfortable during your Reiki session. The moment you feel even the slightest discomfort, you should inform your practitioner. You may be shy or extremely introverted, so the session needs to be modified accordingly. What is more, it is safe to assume you will feel more at ease as you continue on your spiritual journey. Every session will bring you closer to your goal, opening new horizons for you.

The whole process of passing on the knowledge from the Reiki master to the student is called attunement. It is true that you cannot teach yourself Reiki, no matter how hard you try. Of course, you can read all about it, and you can understand the basic principles. However, if you want the full Reiki experience, then you need to turn to a sensei, or else a Reiki master. Then, you will be attuned, in a form of sacred initiation. The master's knowledge will be transferred to you, through the channeling of energy. This is a wonderful sensation, sought after by Reiki students from all over the world.

When you start Reiki sessions, sometimes you become overly enthusiastic about what is going to happen. In your life, you have experienced many negative incidents. You have gone through rough times, overcoming hardships and dealing with things that have changed your point of view. It takes time to heal these wounds and restore your inner balance. This cannot be felt right from the start. On the contrary, you should give yourself time. It is an important step you have taken, so do not rush into it. The benefits will definitely come up, sooner or later.

Some people experience no actual difference in the way they feel after the session. This is one of the major reasons for disappointment. But one of the Reiki principles is relevant to grounding yourself. You need to be grounded, before you reach new heights. How can you fly, when your wings have not fully grown yet? There is a continuum in the various stages of treatment. Think of it as a journey to catharsis. You cannot purify your body, your mind, and your soul, unless you get into the process of cleansing everything around you. It requires time to do so.

This is where you need to have faith and resist the temptation of quitting. Keep in mind that you may even feel discomfort during the session. This does not necessarily mean that your journey toward energy flow restoration will be equally hard along the way. Not at all. It is just the fact that people react differently under specific conditions. Your reaction was such that alarmed you, because your body was in shock. Maybe it is the intensity of the energy that surprised you. Whatever it was, next time you will do better. Your body will be better prepared, which means that your reactions will be milder.

CHAPTER 3
REIKI AS FORM OF TREATMENT

Does Reiki go against what you have grown up to believe about Western medicine? Do you think that medication is the only way to treat disease, disorders, and health problems arising in your life? I am sure you don't, otherwise you would not be here, exploring the wonderful world of Reiki. Well, medicine has come a long way, nobody can argue with that. It is an amazing thing to know that mankind has found the cure for severe health problems of the past. Our quality of life has improved dramatically, through the use of antibiotics, vitamins, and supplements.

At the same time, technology has achieved greatness through the invention of machinery, along with infrastructure, which can be crucial in the health industry. All that is lovely and depicts the magnitude of man's power. However, everything comes with its limitations. Is medicine enough? Unfortunately, not. There are times when doctors cannot do anything but take a step back and hope for the best. There are many cases of patients treated with disease that do not receive the anticipated outcome. On the contrary, they are left to suffer. Not intentionally, of course. But still, it is devastating to see people suffering from a lack of alternatives in treatment.

Reiki has come to fill that gap and offer a new perspective in the health industry. No one can claim to hold the scepter of universal knowledge in treating people. I wish things were that simple. Nonetheless, Reiki provides patients with a new way of encountering disease. It acts as a complementary form of treatment to the conventional methods used by doctors in hospitals all around the world. Reiki is noninvasive, which means its benefits are mild, subtle, yet impressive. Through this holistic experience triggering the spirit, the patient receives a new dynamic way of dealing with illness.

Some might say that conventional medicine is the key to recovery. Nevertheless, this is not always the case. There are patients with severe energy blocks, people who have been psychologically injured who cannot cope with the challenges in their life. Furthermore, there are patients who have been receiving treatment for chronic pain, those undergoing chemotherapy, and many others who feel like they deserve more than what they currently get. This is where Reiki steps in, offering an additional weapon in the patients' arsenal, so as to fight for their well-being.

What Reiki does is target the body, the mind, and the emotional state of the patient. Unlike conventional medicine, Reiki will not heal a specific disease separately from the rest of the entity. Instead, by restoring the energy flow, Reiki will benefit the patient as a whole. Needless to say, there needs to be a strong bond between Reiki and Western medicine. In fact, many hospitals have started incorporating Reiki at their premises. They have accepted the value of such a holistic, spiritual journey for the patient. Rather than condemning alternative treatments, they have acknowledged the benefits that might derive from their use.

Obviously, things have not always been like that. In the past, people looked down on alternative treatments from East Asia. They were afraid because they did not know anything about them. In fact, they were skeptical to trust an entirely different point of view, health wise. It is very easy to criticize others, instead of listening to what they have to say. Perhaps it was also the fact that the Western world saw it as some sort of competition. For all these reasons, treatments such as meditation, acupuncture, aromatherapy, and Reiki did not receive the recognition that they should have from the beginning.

However, as time went by and more people turned to these health treatment options, nobody could ignore the results. That feeling of absolute calmness, an overall positive way of thinking, the lifted spirits, and the increased energy, these are all elements that play an important role in the prognosis of a patient. Reiki has had a tremendous impact on patients, who feel better, and recover more quickly when combining their conventional treatment with this hands-on healing technique.

Nowadays, biased opinions have started vanishing into thin air. It is the perfect time to delve in the eternal power of universal life energy. Scientists do not oppose Reiki, nor could they, even if they tried. Although research on Reiki health benefits is still minimal, the results for the patients speak much louder than words. Reiki no longer begs for a spot in medicine. By bridging the gaps between spirituality and science, Reiki is a great way to boost your inner energy, feel better, and live life more positively. Who wouldn't want that?

Using Reiki to Treat Disease

After having clarified that Reiki does not act independently in treating disease, now let's see where it can help us out toward feeling better. First and foremost, Reiki is an exceptional means of reinforcing a patient's energy flow. This means that the patient will experience the unblocking of glitched energy centers throughout the body. By restoring these energy centers, balance comes next. The patient feels more in sync, without the usual weight preventing them from feeling invigoration. Then, it is that precious sensation of tranquility that surrounds the patient. This is amazing, since many of the aftereffects of disease are related to stress. Reiki is able to deal with stress, conquering the battle of anxiety and allowing the patient to be at ease.

Relaxation is not the only benefit you get from Reiki

sessions. Even though it is one of the major perks, there are many other things to look out for during the attunement. If a patient has been suffering from a compromised immune system, then Reiki can help out a great deal. Even if you are healthy, you will instantly feel a boost in your energy levels through Reiki sessions. It all boils down to the passing of life's energy to your body, through the Reiki practitioner, who will act as the conduit or the mediator, if you will. Imagine how beneficial this energy boost is going to be to those whose immune system has made them prone to illness.

Another benefit strongly correlated to Reiki is the deep detoxification of the body. Our body is filled with toxins and unhealthy elements that we need to get rid of. Reiki teaches the body to be in perfect harmony with nature. On the contrary, all these things that poison us and take their toll on our health are swiped away, leaving us cleansed. You need to come closer to nature, as you are part of it. So, Reiki introduces you to a way of living that balances you inside and out and motivates you to stay true to your cause of a healthy lifestyle.

There are cases of chronic conditions and more acute treatments that may also benefit from Reiki. Patients who undergo radiation, chemotherapy, and dialysis have a profound need for support. By spiking their energy levels and making them feel better, Reiki sessions are crucial to those patients. It is a fact that patients who come to their treatments with a lifted spirit generally enjoy a better prognosis over time. When you are down, drained of energy, overly stressed, and disappointed, you immediately reflect all that pessimism into your body. It is just like a self-fulfilling prophecy. You attract what you are thinking of, instead of what you are supposed to attract (Schaedig, 2020).

In an emergency, your body is under attack. You feel like you are in shock, unable to process what is happening. When it comes to urgent matters, it makes perfect sense to trust conventional medicine, at least at the beginning. A patient might need to undergo surgery, in order to treat an injured limb, a leg, or an arm. In addition, there are cases when patients need transfusion or stitches—a long list of treatments meant to offer comfort, and eventually cure.

However, when the first wave has passed, there is a need for the body to experience an overall sense of recovery. Reiki provides the patient with a soothing experience, targeting the body, the mind, and the soul. The outcome leaves no room for speculation, as the patient enjoys a quicker, more efficient recovery. Bones heal faster, wounds mend more deeply, bruises disappear, and pain management is entirely different. Patients report having wider tolerance and feeling better over time. This is one of the major indications that Reiki works, directly affecting the quality of life for each patient.

Other diseases where Reiki contributes positively include digestion issues, as well as autoimmune health conditions. Patients suffering from such health problems find themselves in a vicious cycle. They do not feel well, which results in experiencing even worse symptoms, and often fueling the disease itself. For instance, colitis, psoriasis, dyspepsia—these are all issues strongly linked to the patient mindset. When the patient finds a way to dispose of stress and depression, their progress is spectacular.

In a world where obesity has become an epidemic, it is only fair to assume that everyone around the globe is searching for a viable solution. Since traditional approaches to fight the weight that has been piling up for so long seem to be unable to deal with the matter effectively, diverse options need to be found. This is the main reason why so many people have turned to alternative treatments, which treat conditions such as obesity in a holistic manner.

When it comes to weight loss, Reiki can help out when combined with healthy eating and moderate exercise. Patients who have no intention of changing their lifestyle will not enjoy any real, long-term benefits from Reiki, as far as weight loss is concerned. Again, Reiki is not a magic pill. What it can do for those who have been struggling to lose weight is to help them address the emotional hardships that often manifest themselves in the process. For example, overconsumption of food often stems from feelings of self-worth or psychological triggers that need to be defined.

What is more, it is important for every patient to love themselves, no matter how much they weigh. The feeling of guilt is usually disastrous, as it prevents personal growth. If a person feels like they cannot accomplish anything in life, then that takes its toll on their mood. How can that very same person commits to a highly demanding diet plan, followed by a consistent workout regime to reach a healthy BMI? This is going to be a bumpy road, and the patient will definitely need all the help they can get.

It is a chain of reactions, all deriving from an emotional imbalance. Reiki can help patients look at the problem without any psychological distractions. Once they have got the strength needed to proceed with the change, the results will be impressive. Through the use of energy fields, the patient will be empowered to set out on a greatly rewarding process. Without that level of help, most people will end up tormenting themselves and sacrificing their health state in the long run. When you do not address the imbalances within your body, you only prolong the inevitable, and it is only a matter of time before you fall back into the same bad habits.

There is a growing interest in Reiki as a form of treatment for patients suffering from cancer. Although no one claims that Reiki can cure such a disease on its own, there have been several observations that regard Reiki as a great complementary treatment. It is true that the psychology of the patient plays a tremendous part in the outcome. Reiki can help with the improvement of the quality of life for patients suffering from cancer, allowing them to experience mental clarity, minimize the pain that they feel, and enjoy life more.

When you have been diagnosed with cancer, your entire life changes. You feel out of balance, because everything around you adjusts to your current needs. Some people find it extremely hard to cope with these changes in their life, as they are afraid, they will lose part of their former identity. Fortunately, Reiki stimulates the energy centers within the body, enabling energy to flow in harmony. This alone fills patients with hope, as they feel it deep within them that they have the power to overcome the problems coming their way. Obviously, this is huge; cancer does not go away on wishful thinking. Yet, it is important to optimize the life quality of the patient, and Reiki is a wonderful addition to cancer treatment.

In a nutshell, Reiki can help patients overcome their health struggles. It does not claim to hold the secret of all healing. Medicine is a well-respected science, which has made groundbreaking discoveries over the years. However, Reiki is an indispensable component of a complete, holistic health treatment. Patients who add Reiki into their daily routine acknowledge its importance and continue Reiki sessions even after their treatment has finished.

Some of the diseases or chronic conditions where Reiki has been proven to work effectively include the following:

- stress, anxiety, panic attacks, psychological issues
- insomnia, difficulty in sleeping
- digestive problems
- headaches
- respiratory conditions
- autoimmune diseases
- depression
- chronic pain
- aftereffects of chronic treatments (chemotherapy, radiation, etc.)
- cancer

The best thing that you can do is discuss with your Reiki practitioner any questions you have as to how to incorporate Reiki into your conventional treatment plan. Many doctors have agreed to use alternative treatments to support the main frame of treatment. A holistic plan increases the chances of success, while at the same time providing great benefits in the emotional and mental health of the patient. In addition, pain relief is real. Many patients have reported a dramatic drop in the intensity of pain experienced, which is of paramount importance.

Even though in the past, conventional treatments and alternative medicine were somewhat contradictory to each other, this breach has been mended. Patients can now combine parts of treatments, according to their individualized needs. There is no limitation, as long as the treatment benefits the patient.

Reiki Principles to Live by

In order to make the most of Reiki as a form of treatment, you must first understand its fundamental principles. Reiki is an entire philosophy, a system believing in the life force energy surrounding the universe. Unless you fully comprehend what it means to pursue absolute harmony with nature, unless you realize that you are not isolated from the world around you, it is difficult to pull through. This is why patients, just like any Reiki student, must understand the five Reiki principles to adhere to in their life.

Of course, these principles have not been conceived as a form of restraining people's lives. They are not limiting at all. On the contrary, they allow the student to acquire a new perspective on life. Reiki acts as a breath of fresh air, a new dynamic way of life, where everything is in sync. This is an instruction manual for happiness, a remedy for the soul. Who doesn't want to be happy? It seems so simple, yet many of us forget all about it.

So, let's have a look at these five Reiki principles, to understand what we need to change in our daily routine:

- First of all, you need to stop worrying. There are things in life nobody can control. What's the point in worrying about these things, other than feeling stressed? You tend to overanalyze every situation, which can be catastrophic for our mentality. By building different scenarios in our mind, we consume valuable energy. This energy should be reserved for the things that actually matter. Instead of worrying, understand what is going on in your life. Assess the situation, and act accordingly. That's it!
- Another crucial principle in the whole Reiki philosophy is not to be angry. Anger is a negative feeling, affecting your inner balance. When you feel anger, you cannot concentrate on anything else. It eats you up, keeping you fixated on the very same thing you should avoid. Try to reach to the source of your anger, encounter it

efficiently and then let go. When you do, you will be thrilled to see how much easier it is to invite happiness in your life. You are not angry; hence, you are not poisoned by negative energy.

- Being modest, and humble is one more thing to consider. This is the third principle—teaching you not to brag. I get it, we all have our personal victories. There is no reason why you should not give credit to yourself for what you have accomplished so far. However, do not forget to be grateful for everything in your life. Be grateful for what you have received and for all those opportunities that have allowed you to shine. You are not alone in the world, do not forget about it.

- Honesty is a virtue in every culture. By lying to others or to yourself, you basically prolong the inevitable. There is no way truth does not reveal itself in the end. So, why waste all this energy, trying to figure out schemes to conceal the truth? Be honest, so that you can always be conscious of reality. Do not lie, as this is not a behavior you would welcome from others. Stop doing the things that bother you, in order to promote similar behavior from the rest of the world. After all, it is all "quid pro quo" (Hayes, n.d.), and you need to accept that.

- Practice compassion with everyone around you, including yourself. This means you should not be cruel with others. Try to get in their shoes, so you understand why they act the way they do. Compassion is a wonderful thing in life. Do not be rigid, since not everything is as it seems. There are many different sides to the story, which is what you need to keep in mind. People act in mysterious ways, although there are always justifications, reasons, and ulterior motives for doing so. The same applies to your behavior.

It is interesting to point out the fact that Reiki focuses on a single day. When you abide by the Reiki principles, you are welcome to do so "just for today." This is very important, as it does not represent a huge commitment. Instead, Reiki teaches you to appreciate the moment. You should not consume your precious energy in anticipation of the future. Nor should you cry over what has happened in the past. You are here now, and this is all that matters. So, your efforts must be focused on the present moment. In this way, you are 100% committed to your life. You feel lighter, healthier, and happier.

One thing that comes to mind when one thinks of Reiki is "impossible." How can someone be that good all the time? What happens when you get an emotional slipup, or when you behave in a way that does not match with your Reiki principles? Does all the hard work you have put into improving your energy flow go to waste? If it does, who can claim to be completely virtuous all the time, without any poisoning thoughts or behavioral patterns that keep them off course?

On the bright side, there is no judgment in Reiki. Even if you fail one day, you are more than welcome to try again. Since you take it one day at a time, this means that you have endless opportunities to make it happen. No one can claim to be realistic, unless they take into consideration the occasional slipup in their life. By introducing Reiki into your daily routine, you have made the first step. It is in your hands how to play along but remember that everyone makes mistakes. As long as you acknowledge them, you will benefit from Reiki.

Your efforts are cumulative, which means that you should not feel sad about having a bad day. It is only human, and you are human. Provided that you accept the fact that we are all flawed, you can compartmentalize and deal with just one day. When you are done, you place your focus on the next day. Before you know it, this small change has affected your entire worldview and has lifted a substantial weight off your chest. Rather than worrying about every single thing that you do in life, start small. Cut yourself some slack and remember that every day is a new blessing for you to show the world what you are made of...as simple as that!

CHAPTER 4
CHAKRAS

Divine energy is omnipresent in the world. Some people call it "Ki" or "Chi," whereas others refer to it as "Prana" or even as "The Holy Spirit." All these terms manifest the exact same essence. Universal energy appears in different cultures, and people praise its glory. Would you ever consider the world without it? It would not be the same, not at all. In fact, energy is the very fabric keeping the universe from falling apart and collapsing. It is its very heart and soul. So, it is only fair that we try to comprehend its essence.

In ancient Japan and the cultures of East Asia, people have managed to glimpse the magnitude of divine energy, in pursuit of fully experiencing the absolute balance from within. They have tried to figure out how to reach the deepest levels of consciousness and relaxation. What they have revealed after thorough research and close observation is that a universal energy flow influences us all. There is a strong bond between us, keeping us connected with the rest of the world. According to the quality of this energy flow, people get to feel happy or sad. They get to experience emotions and enjoy life differently.

Chakras depict just that. They are called "wheels of life" because they represent the various energy centers within our body (Zoldan, 2020). If energy runs smoothly through these energy centers, then we feel happy and blessed. In the unfortunate event there is a block in one of these centers, however, everything falls apart. Obviously, a single center affects the entire body. The much anticipated balance vanishes, and instead you experience the aftermath of an imbalanced entity. The feeling is chaotic, and unless you deal with it effectively, the discomfort will only become stronger over time.

On the bright side, our energy centers can be remedied. They are not static. Although it requires a lot of work, you can restore the energy levels within your body. After that, you need to make sure that your energy keeps flowing smoothly, in balance with the universe. Otherwise, you will be simply trying to avoid something bound to happen again and again. So, if you are conscious of the importance of proper energy pulsating through you, then you ought to clear your chakras. These wheels of life need to be in a pristine state at all times. Your well-being depends on them.

Chakras originated from the Tantric philosophy in India, many centuries ago. A lot of different cultures have adopted the same concept, which brings us to the growing interest of the Western world in that. Yoga as we know it all over the world acknowledges the seven energy centers (or chakras) within our body. Nevertheless, there is a huge misconception that many people tend to believe. There is a widespread conviction that the energy centers resemble our body parts. Sometimes people try to figure out where exactly they are located, missing out on the essence of these chakras. They are fluid, rather than statically positioned somewhere. So, if you are wasting a lot of energy in search of the exact location of your chakras, don't.

In fact, several different types of chakras have been created over the years. You can find a system of five, six, seven, or more chakras within the body. We have agreed to use the seven-chakra system in the Western world, as a point of reference. In addition, these seven chakras are accurate representations of where your energy can be found. Even though certain philosophies often report up to 16 different chakras, seven are sufficient.

Below, I am going to show you these chakras around the body, explaining how each of them affects our body in a specific manner. Once you become accustomed to their location and their value, feel free to practice Reiki sessions to unblock any abnormalities in their energy flow.

Energy Fields Around the Body

Before moving forward with chakras, let's talk about another field of energy located in our body. There is a bright light surrounding the physical body, almost like an egg-like cocoon. This cocoon accompanies people from the moment of their birth until their dying breath. It is called an aura and actually consists of seven different layers. All these layers are made of varying intensity energy. The aura is just like a protective shield for you. It is important to keep in mind the fact that the size of your aura is not always the same. On the contrary, it changes depending on certain factors, including your overall well-being.

Your aura is omnipresent, meaning that you can be sure that it never goes away throughout your life. Hence, you can detect the aura in a number of ways. There are digital representations for you to seek, where you can actually see your aura and understand all the slightest details. In addition, you may want to use accessories, such as a pendulum, in order to detect your aura. However, even if you cannot see tangible evidence, it is still there. Take a moment and close your eyes. Even if you cannot immediately remember realizing the existence of your aura, I am sure that you will eventually. Have you ever felt like you have eyes in the back of your head? How can you explain that feeling of awareness? Trust me, it's there! The most striking thing to consider is that you can even feel it with your hands— you just need to reach out and give it some time.

Complementary to the existence of aura, there are seven distinct chakras all over the body, from the spine to the top of the head. Of course, these energy centers need to be aligned for the perfect energy flow to be accomplished. Even a single blockage might jeopardize your entire endeavor, which is a shame. You are welcome to experiment with identifying your energy centers, trying to understand how the energy flows through them.

Root Chakra

First off, there is the Root Chakra. You may have seen it in pictures, and it is located right on the base of your spine. The Root Chakra is a red color, and it has to do with the feeling of trust you have cultivated in the world. Are you afraid of trusting others? Then this is something to work on with the Root Chakra. Through this basic energy center, you become confident enough to trust in your power and claim what is yours. When the energy runs smoothly here, you can stand upright and show others what you are made of, claiming your position in the world. It keeps you grounded but at the same time lets nobody take advantage of you. As long as the energy in this chakra is balanced, you are never the victim. You are present in the moment, confident, and independent.

Sacral Chakra

Moving a little further upward in the body, we run into the Sacral Chakra. This is the second energy center, spotted in the abdomen. This is orange in color, representing sexuality, creativity, and emotional balance. If energy is abundant in this center, then you feel accomplished and satisfied in your life. You are able to create, gather inspiration, and fulfill your dreams. Nonetheless, if there are issues relevant to the energy flow in the Sacral Chakra, then many negative feelings spring out to threaten your well-being. You may experience jealousy, problems with your self-esteem, or a feeling of inadequacy, and you never cease to feel hungry for more. Finally, sex fulfillment has to do with the energy balance in this chakra.

Solar Plexus Chakra

The Solar Plexus Chakra is the third in line. As its name suggests, it is located in the solar plexus. It is yellow, just like the rays of the sun. If you often feel indecisive, then maybe you need to consider unblocking the energy flow in this center. This specific chakra reflects your ability to take initiative and believe in yourself. It offers you the opportunity to show off your individual strength and your willingness to prevail. When there is an imbalance in the Solar Plexus Chakra, you usually feel it in your body as self-doubt. Moreover, perhaps you experience digestive issues, or problems in the stomach, the gallbladder, or even the liver. This chakra depicts your intellectual worth. If you do not believe in yourself and your worth as a human being, then it makes sense you suffer from severe energy flow matters in this very center.

Heart Chakra

Green in color, the Heart Chakra is responsible for matters of the heart. Love, compassion, spirituality, and emotional wellness—these are what the Heart Chakra regulates. Located in the middle of your chest, exactly where the heart is, this energy center is of immense value. Without it, you cannot expect to let go of your guard and love unconditionally. You cannot expect to feel compassion about anyone else. Empathy is a virtue, and you can only acquire it through the Heart Chakra. You will experience grief, uncontrollable sadness, or depression, unless you deal with the matters of the heart. On the other hand, once you do, your heart will be filled with light and joy. Physically, it is not rare for people suffering from imbalances in this very center to also suffer from heart disease. So, you can see why it is of the essence to restore your energy flow here and promote emotional healing.

Throat Chakra

The Throat Chakra is blue in color, and you can find it at the throat. Its main function is communication, which is the key to successful interpersonal relationships. If there are problems with the energy flow in this center, you will most likely experience a difficulty in expressing yourself. You will find it hard to communicate with others or convey the messages you want to, and this can lead to havoc. It is only fair to assume that lack of communication results in an inability to listen to others. This comes across as selfishness and causes breaches in relationships. As a consequence, you might experience hostility and feel isolated. On a physical level, the Throat Chakra is associated with problems in the dental area, as well as the respiratory system.

Third Eye Chakra

We move upward and reach the Third Eye Chakra. This is located on the head, right above the eyebrows and in between the eyes. Its color is indigo, and it is responsible for your awareness. When it functions properly, this energy center allows you to contact your spiritual self. This is the source of intuition, mental clarity, and clairvoyance. If you want to dream without limits and manifest those dreams into actions, then you need to clear out any imbalance of your Third Eye Chakra. You must keep the third eye open, so as to allow your spiritual awakening. When there are problems with this energy center, you can expect to suffer from severe headaches, anxiety, and trouble sleeping. Once the energy flow is restored, though, you will notice a significant improvement and forget all about insomnia. This is one of the reasons why so many people turn to Reiki in the first place.

Crown Chakra

Last but definitely not least, on the top of your head you will find the Crown Chakra. This is the seventh energy center of your body, and it is violet in color. This is the energy center leading to spirituality. If you are searching for that deep connection with the universe, then the Crown Chakra is what you should consider. Some people believe this is the exact place where the physical and spiritual world become one. If the Crown Chakra functions as it should, you enjoy spiritual clarity and deeper understanding of the world. You are in perfect alignment with the universe, and you appreciate the harmony in nature. Otherwise, you lack certainty, and you do not believe in yourself. You are constantly struggling to compare yourself to others, and you feel lonely all the time.

As you can see, the seven energy centers of your body reflect the balance of your body parts. If you want to feel happy and be healthy, then you need to pay attention to this holistic approach. Reiki allows you to unblock any imbalances and restore smooth energy flow from within. This in turn makes your body flourish, freeing your mind and enabling you to connect with your spiritual self. It is a chain of reactions, which otherwise compromise your well-being.

The Reiki practitioner will channel the energy throughout your body, rebalancing its flow in a way that comforts and relieves you from any pain or discomfort. There may or may not be touching. This depends solely on the practitioner. Another important aspect of the Reiki experience, however, is the use of Reiki images. These symbols are optional, as they are not sacred per se. Still, the Reiki master may charge them accordingly, in order to enhance the benefits derived from the process. So, which are the most frequently used Reiki symbols?

Reiki Symbols & Images

Reiki healers transmit the energy of the universe from their palms to their students by using the seven energy centers of their bodies. There is no fixed way to do so, as the attunement (this is what the whole process is called) itself does not have set steps to complete. It is not rare for Reiki practitioners to use various symbols from the philosophical scope of Reiki, in order to enhance the spiritual experience. When they do, these symbols turn into vessels. The practitioners move their palms, mentally recreating the specific symbol they have in their mind. In this way, they boost its healing properties.

There are different ways for you to pass on the power of these symbols during your Reiki session. One way is for you to draw the symbol, using your thumb, your index finger, and middle finger. Of course, you do not need to have a pen or any drawing equipment with you. You are not going to write anything. However, this technique enables you to make the symbol present. Alternatively, you can visualize it. This requires a little more familiarization with the symbols, but it works wonders when you are a seasoned Reiki healer. Whatever you choose to do, it is important to repeat the symbol's name three times. This will help you feel its presence and enhance its powerful properties. Below, I am going to explain to you the most popular Reiki symbols, which can be used during your healing session.

First of all, there is the Power Symbol. This is one of the fundamental symbols in the philosophy of Reiki. It is basically a coil. It forms a spiral line, resembling a snail. Think of a staircase, starting at the top floor and going all the way down to the basement. On top, there will be lighter. In contrast, at the bottom you will find no light whatsoever. In a similar pattern, this symbol is used to adjust the power of the energy. Depending on whether or not you are looking for more intense light in your life, the Reiki healer will move their palms creating that symbol.

Another great symbol in the Reiki experience is the Distance Symbol. When you draw this, you will immediately think that it is a pagoda. It looks like a tower, while its formation clearly creates distance between the Reiki student and anything on their mind. So, this symbol is perfect when encountering problems with other people, and with issues of intimacy and hardships in forming relationships. Through the Distance Symbol, people are brought closer to each other, minimizing the barriers formed before them.

The Harmony Symbol is next in line. There are two ways of looking at it. Most people will agree that its shape resembles that of a wave fiercely touching the shore. However, some others claim that this symbol represents a flying bird's wing. You are free to decide which interpretation is best for you. When you have problems with depression, stress, extreme sadness, and loneliness, such a symbol can boost the healing properties of Reiki, offering you the opportunity to balance your emotions. You will find mental clarity, away from the negative feelings you have experienced in the past. This symbol can contribute to a quicker recovery.

These three symbols combined form another symbol, which is only used between Reiki healers during the attunement. More specifically, the Master Symbol is a combination of the three previously mentioned symbols. It promotes enlightenment, encompassing the very essence of Reiki. It is not simple at all, which explains why its use is limited to Reiki masters. Its power is immense, as it combines three different symbols. Its function is harmony, as the Reiki healer anticipates passing on the path to mental and spiritual balance.

Finally, there is the Completion Symbol. When you see it for the first time, you will think it is lightning. Once you have received the energy of the universe, you are now in need of grounding. This is where the Completion Symbol comes along, upon finishing the Reiki session. Your energy has been restored and is now invited to stay within you. The direction of the lightning is from up to the ground and not the other way around. In this way, you regain your connection with the world. You are a part of the universe, and you are in absolute harmony with your surroundings.

Having forged a path with the symbols used in Reiki, now it is high time we focused more on the images. In order to enhance the intensity of the Reiki session, you need to visualize several images and keep them in mind. These images will act as a form of inspiration, motivating you to take a leap of faith and travel through space and time. A great picture can speak louder than a thousand words, right? These images are quite fluid, and each Reiki practitioner brings to mind things that make them feel pleasant.

If you are interested in patterns, then you will be thrilled to know more about how these images are selected in the first place. They are images, depicting landscapes promoting relaxation. Where do you feel utterly relaxed? Which place makes you feel lighter than a feather? Keep asking these questions, and the answers will appear before your eyes. There are places of unbounded beauty in the world. Waterfalls, evergreen plains, emblematic mountains, the seashore, and so much more can serve as a source of inspiration to us all. Watching the sunset by the beach or enjoying a sunrise from the peak of a mountain sounds idyllic. It is equally remarkable to relish the sight of a cherry blossom tree, a field of daisies, or a cloudless sky.

Another popular theme in Reiki images is that of celestial objects. You are trying to connect with the universe, so visualizing a constellation or the vastness of the universe can perform true miracles in your spiritual journey. Wonderful chromatic panels, shades highlighting the beauty of the world, are blended with the floating presence of the planets, the stars, and everything in between. Such images allow you to elevate the entire experience, which is obviously a good thing.

Along with the images, you should consider the musical

background. Some images are so powerful that they enable you to travel through the dimensions in a heartbeat. Nevertheless, it is amazing what you can accomplish through the proper combination between an image and sounds. For example, the sound of the waves gently touching the shore awakens the senses. Tree leaves, birds humming, soft music, even cymbals, the flute, or the sound of bells—these are all fabulous ways to take your experience to a whole new level.

Apart from anything else, you can use online resources to enrich your experience. There are a wide variety of videos on the web, and you can turn to them for inspiration. A video usually consists of several images. Sometimes it also features mottos and inspirational mantras. In videos, you can find symbols, as well as colorful combinations that induce deep relaxation. On top of all that, of course, the right music that completes the experience in the most spectacular manner.

Whatever you choose to use during your Reiki session, you need to be honest with yourself. Find the images that work best for you and experiment with different themes. In this way, you will see which images you are most receptive to and which ones do not trigger any results. Even if you enjoy an image aesthetically, this does not mean that the specific image is good Reiki-wise. Therefore, you need to try out various images. Your reactions to them will show you which way to go. Once you have found it, you can either use the same image in each session or change.

CHAPTER 5
ENHANCING YOUR REIKI EXPERIENCE

Reiki itself is absolutely fabulous as a holistic treatment that keeps you aligned with the universe. It offers you the chance to restore your inner balance through the smooth energy flow that runs from within you. However, Reiki should not be used on its own. If you are looking for the maximum effects, then you need to combine Reiki along with some targeted exercises, enabling you to strengthen your body and keep fit. Once you have started this great combo of wellness, you will immediately notice the difference. Your mindset will be even clearer, and you will feel lighter and be filled with energy to keep running through your day.

If you are looking for a New Year's resolution, there is nothing better than to embark on this spiritual journey, which will benefit you in more ways than you can imagine. As the year comes to an end, it is only fair to reminisce about the moments that made us feel good. At the same time, we tend to be harsh with ourselves regarding the moments where we believe we were wrong. As a result, we want to escape this vicious cycle of moderation. Instead, we want to experience something out of the ordinary. We know now is the time for generous decisions, which will change the course of our life and lead us to a higher level of understanding.

Of course, many New Year's resolutions are only valid for a couple of weeks. After the first excitement comes the devastating realization that everything is "easier said than done." So, most people start the new year filled with hope that something is about to change. They make the necessary preparations, and then they realize it takes more than that. They need to commit long term, in order to enable change. Otherwise, it is plain as day that their ventures are about to fail. I hope Reiki is not just a whim for you. If it is, I suggest you looked for something less demanding to begin with— Reiki is not a fad.

"Mens sana in corpore sano" or "A sound mind in a sound body" (Ancient Olympics, n.d.). First and foremost, you ought to remember that. You cannot expect to have proper balance, without focusing on your body, as well as your spirit. In order to do that, there are several things that you can do. You can try out different forms of mild workout, which allow you to strengthen your muscles, increase your flexibility, and remain active throughout the day. It doesn't have to be something extreme, like going to the gym on a daily basis. I know most people cannot, and will not, adhere to such rigid plans. However, you can incorporate kundalini yoga or meditation, as well as reflexology, in your daily regimen.

Along with that, you need to find the right Reiki exercises that help you with your intentions. According to what you want to accomplish, you should adjust your Reiki session and boost the results you have dreamt of getting through this spiritual journey. This is a fluid experience, which can be tailor made to suit your own needs. If you feel like you want to concentrate more on a single body organ or a specific behavioral pattern, then you can target that rather than consume energy through generic exercises. Reiki is not a "one-size-fits-all" solution, after all.

Of course, it is equally important to live by the Reiki principles. If you want to feel the magnitude of universal life energy, then you must synchronize yourself with it. Unless you get rid of the negativity and the problems that are dragging you down and keeping you away from nature's bliss, you will not enjoy the full Reiki experience. So, be sure to spend each day feeling grateful for your many blessings, compassionate toward yourself and others, humble and grounded, calm, and honest. These things might seem trivial, yet they play an important role in your mental clarity, as much as your emotional health.

Even if you have great intentions to thrive in life, sadly you cannot do it on Reiki alone. A holistic treatment would not have it any other way, right? One of the vital parts of this journey is to treat your body as if it were a shrine. To that end, you need to improve your diet. It doesn't matter if you are overweight or if you meet your BMI goals. What matters is that you respect your body, as this is your vessel in the physical world. I am going to come to that later on with some practical tips. However, think of it this way; would you ever expect your vehicle to run on muddy water? I know the answer is evident, but you need to steer clear of those temptations that damage your body and create imbalances with your spirit and mind.

Putting Theory into Practice

First things first. When you want to optimize your Reiki experience, you need to be meticulous. You must have a well-thought-out plan to adhere to, in order to make the most of your efforts. So, instead of deciding to follow the route to spirituality on the spur of the moment, arrange things so that you keep motivated throughout your venture. A journal will come in handy.

A diary of some sort, where you can keep track of your progress—this is particularly important, since you are setting out on a journey in uncharted territories. You do not have any past experience, so you cannot know for sure what works for you and what should change in your routine. By studying your experience day by day, you will gradually understand what you should keep and what you need to alter. This is a trial and error situation, and you learn as you go.

Besides that, I have pointed out earlier in the book that you should make sure to stay active. One of the best ways to do so is by practicing yoga. In fact, it is a great option to practice

Kundalini yoga. As a result, not only will you tone those muscles, shed the extra pounds, and boost your metabolism. At the same time, you will have the opportunity to awaken the powerful Kundalini. This is the ultimate energy of life. It is the feminine energy, in its pure form (Müller, 2020). If you fully comprehend what this means, and you still want to go ahead with awakening this fierce energy from within, then yoga is an excellent way to achieve that.

Kundalini energy remains dormant, located somewhere at the base of your spine. You can trigger its awakening, through the practice of specific yoga poses, such as the Breath of Fire. In this pose, you simply inhale and exhale, maintaining the same level of intensity. You do so multiple times, breathing in and out. As soon as you have found your rhythm, you can breathe more deeply and exhale while placing your arms on either side of your body. Another Kundalini yoga pose is that of Frogs. In this case, you bend your knees, just like a frog would do. Your heels touch the ground. Then, as you inhale, your legs are straight and almost touch each other, while your hips face upward. Your head faces the ground. As you exhale, you return to the initial position.

Once you awaken your Kundalini energy, it is going to be unstoppable. You will not be able to control it, as it flows through your chakras. You will experience it full speed, and the results might even shock you. Nevertheless, you should not be afraid. Some people spend their entire life trying to awaken this spiral-shaped energy force, but they never do. Feel free to open yourself to the opportunity to unravel this mysterious energy, which in turn reveals your true self.

Meditation is another exceptional tool you can use, so as to optimize your Reiki experience. Some people feel that they cannot concentrate enough to indulge in meditation. Yet, there is nothing that you cannot accomplish, once you set your mind on it. Although difficulties will rise along the way, this does not mean that they should prevent you from meditating. In fact, you will see that you become addicted to this time of absolute silence, as soon as you start your sessions. Are you worried about the time? Then, try to make some time! It is hard, I know. We all have a ton of things to do, and 24 hours is just not enough. But you need to try and figure out a viable plan for you.

The simplest way to meditate is by sitting down, with your two hands touching right in front of your chest. You may know this position as the Gassho (or the first pillar of Reiki). This is indeed the prayer position, where you can relax and concentrate on your breathing. Close your eyes and dispose of any thoughts. You should hear nothing but the sound of echoing silence. At first, you will definitely feel uncomfortable. After a while, though, you become accustomed to the silence.

A different approach to meditation is grounding meditation. In this case, you stand up. Once again, you focus on your breathing. Close your eyes. Both your hands are touching your belly, as you start breathing deeply. You inhale and exhale, maintaining a steady pace. In your mind, you repeat your actions. In this, you ground your body and create the conditions allowing you to experience Reiki. After fully connecting with the Earth through this meditation for about 10 minutes, you are ready to place your hands in the Gassho position. Open your eyes and feel the energy overflowing.

For even better results in your overall well-being, reflexology can become part of your daily routine. According to its principles, your palms and feet are a map of your entire body. Each part represents a different body organ, which means that through proper touching, this organ can be stimulated. Obviously, reflexology is a holistic treatment for those who want to enjoy perfect harmony with the environment and nature all around. It is a great way to relieve your body from stress, get rid of toxins, and relax your muscles. Although it is quite different from Reiki itself, in essence each one complements the other. Reflexology provides more practical treatment, while Reiki offers a deeper connection to your spirituality.

Finally, a truly intriguing concept you can add to your morning ritual, or when you have the time, is manifesting. More particularly, the Law of Attraction can be used for you to attract the things that you really want (Rataic, 2016). If you focus on what you want to achieve, your thoughts will reflect what you actually attract over time. Therefore, you must fill your mind with positive thoughts. You should concentrate on the blessings you would like to have in your life, gradually leading them toward you. This concept of manifestation is widely known all over the world. Of course, Reiki offers you the opportunity to relax and get rid of all the toxic thoughts that have been poisoning your life. As a consequence, you make room for the positive outcomes you anticipate coming your way.

By following the guidelines, I have laid out for you here, it is certain that you are going to get the maximum effects of Reiki. In absolute harmony with the universe, you will feel that you belong to an entity so great, so magnificent, so glorious. This is a wonderful sensation, allowing you to reach the deepest level of spirituality in the world. Commit to this experience, and you will be surprised by the benefits.

Healing Crystals

During Reiki sessions, it is often recommended to use healing crystals. These are accessories, which optimize the spiritual experience for the Reiki student. They come in different sizes, colors, and shapes. Each of these crystals targets a specific feature. Crystals have been known since antiquity, and they are important assets in various cultures all around the world for their healing properties. Their powers are controversial, yet a lot of people believe in their mystical powers. In fact, during Reiki you will most likely feel a tingling sensation while using the crystal on one of your energy centers.

It is important to remember that not all crystals are suitable to become part of your Reiki experience. On the contrary, you must decide which crystals to use, based on your intentions. What do you want to achieve through these healing crystals? Once you answer this question, you will know what to bring to your next session. However, you should always trust your instinct. Even if it is not clear why you are drawn to a particular healing crystal, you should try it out and see why your subconscious has arranged for you to get it. You might be surprised by what you discover!

Before looking into the various healing crystals, I wanted to point out the fact that they should be well cared for, from the moment you buy them. I mean, it goes without questioning that the healing crystal will have gathered negative energy all this time. It is your responsibility to cleanse it properly, so it can help you achieve your own goals. That being said, you need to clean the healing crystal with the use of pure water, as soon as you get it home. Get the tap running, and let the cool water perform its miracles. For even better results, you can burn some sage in the room where you are going to store it.

Let's move forward with the identification of some of the world's best healing crystals. My personal favorite is amethyst. This amazingly purple stone targets honesty, along with healing and purification. You can use it to regulate your sleep and get rid of negativity. It is a beautiful stone, offering amazing healing properties. Clear quartz, on the other hand, is transparent. It is often referred to as the "master healer" due to its versatile nature. This precious stone allows you to restore balance, building your immune system and enabling you to reach out to your goals. It is a great healing crystal to keep by your side at all times.

If you are looking for protection, then you should seek obsidian. Its dark color is amazingly addictive, but its impressive function is not limited to just that. What is impressive about obsidian is the fact that it comes from volcanic eruptions, thereby accumulating an immense amount of energy within. Its main healing power is that of protection, which is great. Apart from that, however, you can turn to this stone for mental clarity, and relief from pain. Rose quartz is another favorite stone, pink in color and reflecting love. It helps you regain trust in others and improve your interpersonal relationships. Dealing with trust issues, this healing crystal is exceptionally useful to those who have been hurt in the past and are afraid of letting go again.

Tiger's Eye is perhaps one of the most popular healing crystals you can find in the market. It brings harmony into your life, through its golden color and emblematic formation. If you are feeling dubious of your capabilities, then this will help you dispose of your fears and believe in yourself. This healing crystal will enable you to think clearly and boost your self-confidence to claim what you are entitled to. Moving on, sapphire is a blue crystal reflecting wisdom, as well as affluence. In case you are struggling with your finances and seek some help toward gaining economic power, this is the right stone for you.

Ruby is an exceptional healing crystal that is scarlet red. This is a sexy stone, meant to offer a boost in your sensuality and vitality. If you are in pursuit of improving your sex life, then you should use this stone to lift your libido. At the same time, ruby is excellent in bringing out the truth. In cases of trust issues, you can always turn to this healing crystal for assistance. Then, there is moonstone. This amazingly subtle healing crystal promotes inner growth and offers you the chance to start over fresh. Are you tired of the way your life has been so far? Are you craving a change? This is the best thing to keep within your grasp, so as to attract exactly what you want in your life.

Bloodstone will make you stronger, which is a great thing to do. We would all welcome a powerful boost in our life, right? Its dark green color is intoxicating, while its properties are endless. You can count on the bloodstone for aligning yourself with nature and the environment. This healing crystal will allow you to relax, invigorate, awaken your senses, and get rid of negative thoughts altogether. Finally, I would like to wrap up my detailed analysis of healing crystals with citrine. This is a lovely healing crystal, aiming at optimism. Are you feeling down? Then, you should buy this precious stone and watch as the negative thoughts leave your mind. If you are looking for that spark of joy, you know where to look!

All these crystals optimize your Reiki experience and introduce you into the powerful properties of precious possessions. Even though they are not essential parts of the Reiki process, I would advise you to get your hands on a couple of those crystals. As soon as you bring them close, you will feel differently. Their impact is invaluable, intense, and impressive. Your spirit will be lifted simply by looking at them. This is not such a trivial thing to consider, right? Whatever makes your day even a little more enjoyable is great, and you should make sure to surround yourself with things that boost your mood.

Apart from being beautiful and radiant with a positive energy vibe, these healing crystals can act as a form of visualization for the Reiki healer. In addition, they get rid of the negative energy all around you. So, you get a win-win situation, where you no longer poison yourself with toxicity, and you are flooded with positive energy that will transform your life. How cool is that, especially stemming from a single item? It is no wonder why people have realized the power of crystals ever since ancient times, in many different cultures of the world.

CHAPTER 6
ANECDOTAL STORIES AND CASE EXAMPLES

What is your personal experience with Reiki? Have you ever tried it, or is it something entirely new to you? More than that, what has triggered your interest in finding out more about Reiki? There are people who have never heard of this holistic treatment, whereas others have been motivated to see what it is after reading about it online. Furthermore, there are books dedicated to the philosophy of Reiki; shows on TV try to unravel the mysteries of this noninvasive healing perspective from East Asia, while at least some of your acquaintances have tried it out so far.

The truth is that Reiki has gained great popularity over the past few years all over the world, and there is good reason for that. People have been growing more conscious of their well-being, aiming at a healthier and happier lifestyle. Many of us struggle to maintain our inner balance, lost in the chaotic rhythms of modern society. When there is no time to see those, we hold dear to ourselves, when there is no time to enjoy those precious moments together, how can we make time for ourselves?

It is easy to be consumed by the frenzy of modern life. You wake up in the morning feeling stressed, and you lie in your bed at night exhausted. What is strange is that you most likely feel even more stressed, rather than having the satisfaction of accomplishing your goals. Most people tend to add more things to their "to do" list, ending up asphyxiating under the pressure to make it through the day. However, this is not actually "living." This can barely be described as "surviving." How long can you keep up with that, before you realize that something has to change?

Reiki is here to offer you a way out. It is a breath of fresh air, welcoming you to the genuine meaning of life. You no longer have to worry about thousands of different things.

Instead, your main focus should be right here, right now. In this way, you learn to appreciate the moment. You become conscious of the present, which allows you to enjoy every day of your life, away from these sirens of the past. There are no more distractions between yourself and what really matters. Is this something that makes you smile?

The best thing about Reiki is that it is not just another philosophical trend. On the contrary, it is something that you can apply in your life right away. You do not need to think about it for ages, weighing the pros and trying to figure out the cons. This healing process does not require anything from you, besides your commitment to optimize your life. Are you willing to do that? Then you are ready to become part of the Reiki community. It is not mere theory, but rather an easy-to-apply method of treating your body, your mind, and your spirit.

What is more, there are thousands of people out there who have changed their life through Reiki. They have managed to put their concerns behind them and modify the way they think. Once they got out of their comfort zone, once they saw what Reiki is all about, there was no way back. They devoted their life to a noble cause, passing on their acquired knowledge to others, who then found themselves in the same position. Isn't it wonderful? The sense of solidarity between the Reiki master and the student is amazing. It is that solidarity, that feeling of comradery, which has led to an impressive growth in numbers.

Below, I am going to narrate just a few of the case studies which have influenced me a great deal over the years. I have been practicing Reiki for a long time, and I have met a lot of interesting people. Each of them has given me something unique; each has won a special place in my heart. Above all, I am grateful for the opportunity that has been handed out to me, so as to gain invaluable wisdom through observation, communication, and sharing. I hope you find the same level of inspiration through these case studies and motivational stories, to take the leap of faith. It is so worth it—I promise!

Inspirational Case Studies

Reiki is a subtle, yet extremely effective healing treatment. Many people around the world have found in Reiki a new way of dealing with their disease, their emotional issues, and their mental clarity. I have been blessed with meeting remarkable people in their journey toward discovering Reiki. Some of them have stayed with me for a brief amount of time, while others have become close friends—almost family.

I am grateful for all of these experiences, as they have contributed to my present self. Below, I will show you a few of the cases that have made a great impression on me. Maybe you will find similarities with your own self, or perhaps you will get inspired by their strength and courage. Either way, I hope you enjoy reading how Reiki has transformed their life.

Jane A.

I would like to start with a case study dealing with depression and grief. Jane A. suffered a huge personal loss, which was something that she struggled to cope with for a long time. After a loved one passed away, she became an entirely different person. She could not find happiness in anything, not even the things that she enjoyed doing before that unfortunate event. The fact that the loss was sudden only made things worse. Every day, she found herself sinking even deeper into depression, and she did not have the strength to pull through and recover.

Jane was reluctant at first to try out Reiki. She has heard

about it from some friends, but she thought it was just another trend, which would eventually fade away. However, she decided to give it a try, after many arguments with her sister. When she walked through the door, I could see her reluctance. It was written all over her face. I did not want to put any pressure on her, obviously. So, we just sat there for a while, as I explained to her more details about Reiki. She had no clue as to what was going to happen during the session. I tried to be as detailed as possible, so that she would trust in me. I could not proceed otherwise. So, I had to prove to her that Reiki was absolutely safe, and she had nothing to lose.

During the session, I could feel her blockage. It was real, she was suffering. I tried to concentrate on the chakras that had been most affected by the grief she was experiencing. It was intense. On the bright side, she felt a change, and at the end of the session she was eager to book our next appointment. I cannot say that it was easy to let go of the pain and handle the grief. On the bright side, Jane gradually succeeded in turning over a new leaf. She came to terms with that tragic loss, feeling grateful that she had met the person in the first place. She focused on the happy thoughts, the pleasurable moments that she had spent with him. This was the key to restore her inner balance, smoothen the surface, and pave the way for a new beginning.

I will always be thankful to Jane, as she trusted me to help her in her struggles. No matter how much she hurt inside, she was still calling out for someone to show her the way. She wanted to deal with her loss, she wanted to move forward, but she didn't know how. I am very happy to have shown her the way in handling such a huge loss, channeling her energy to fill her with hope, strength, and connection with the spiritual self.

Peter & Kate W.

It is not rare for families to come to a deadlock, consumed in their personal agonies and trying to restore their former balance. This was the case with Kate W. and her son, Peter. Kate was a divorced woman, who was raising Peter alone. There was no contact with the father, and Peter blamed her for that. He did not want to listen to any of her reasons, because he thought that his mother was untrue to him. At the same time, Kate had invested too much emotionally in her son, and this was suffocating him. Since Peter was a teenager, he had severe mood swings, which only made things worse.

As you can imagine, this was an explosive atmosphere for both of them. Kate was very enthusiastic about coming to Reiki sessions, whereas Peter was very introverted and did not think that it would do them any good. Thankfully, they both came. We sat down together, and I tried to be as detailed as I could about the process. I discussed it with them in an honest, straightforward way. There were times when I could feel Peter doubting what I was saying. However, I started having sessions with both of them. The whole experience was bumpy at the beginning. Kate was doing great, but Peter was still holding back, even after three whole sessions.

Suddenly, things changed. I felt his barriers slowly lifting. Peter became friendlier toward me, as he opened up and welcomed the energy flow to his chakras. It was awesome to see a young boy, on his way to adulthood, gradually realizing his power. He let go of the anger he was holding on to and finally managed to discuss it with his mother. This change got them closer together, and they cannot even recall the last time they argued about something.

Family issues can be hard, especially when there are children. Kate and Peter are a lovely example of how much a family can accomplish, as long as there is love and will to cope with the challenges. It is inevitable to face problems along the way. Nobody can avoid them forever. Yet, with proper understanding, everything can be resolved. This family has astounded me, as to how much they can achieve when they stand united, and I feel blessed to have met them.

Madison E.

Autoimmune diseases are extremely difficult to manage in the long run, as they continue on their path and constantly drain the energy of the patient. This is what Madison E. suffered from. She had been diagnosed with rheumatoid arthritis, which caused her severe pain in the joints. Each day was a struggle. She wanted to lift that weight off her shoulders, but she did not know how to do it alone. On the bright side, she experimented with many different treatments because she was convinced that she would find something to comfort her.

I met Madison through a common acquaintance, and I was immediately drawn to her. Even though she was in continuous pain, she managed to smile brightly and light up the room. We decided to practice Reiki sessions, so that she could relieve some of that excruciating pain. From the very first time, I was shocked at the blocks of energy throughout her body. Her joints were clogged, energy could not flow gently. She was tense; her muscles were tight, and you could see her suffer. Fortunately, this was about to change.

Along with Reiki, I suggested therapeutic massage treatments with a special focus on the joints. At the same time, Madison would practice meditation. This allowed her to become even more conscious of the world and her connection with her spirituality. Things got better. Obviously, this disease will always be around. However, I am happy to report that Madison is now in remission. She feels much less pain, and she can walk without collapsing from exhaustion. Her quality of life has improved dramatically, which makes her hope even more for the future.

It is a blessing for me as a Reiki healer to see such a noticeable change in the life of a student. Madison has taught me never to give up, even when things appear to be really bad. There is always hope, and you can always fight to see another day. I keep her in my prayers and send out my love to her, along with my best wishes for a life filled with happiness and love.

Stories to Motivate You to Practice Reiki

There are many people who value helping others. It runs in their blood and fills them with a deep sense of accomplishment. These people have dedicated their life toward assisting others. Sometimes they do that by sacrificing their own well-being. They put the needs of others before their own, even though they could do exactly the opposite. After all, the survival instinct dictates just that; you do whatever it takes to survive. It never mentions the rest of the world, does it?

I have always felt a special kind of connection with these people. I understand what has been driving them in their life, and I sympathize with them. Although I love myself, and I would never do anything to hurt my feelings, jeopardize my well-being, or suffer, I can understand the urge to do so. To some, there is no greater satisfaction than that derived from helping another human being. In my life, I have had the pleasure to meet quite a few of those people. Reiki is a fantastic way of bringing amazing personalities together, joining a community of people who are eager to help and pass on their invaluable wisdom to others.

Laura and Jason are both special, because of their

background. They have come a long way, and they have found their truth in Reiki. Although at first, they experienced quite a few obstacles getting in the way, in the end they found peace. They found their calling, which made them both so happy and complete. Let's read about their story, shall we?

Laura K.

Laura is an incredible woman, who has always felt a little awkward about her intuition. She sensed things differently, and most people considered her too sensitive. In fact, this was the reason her family had tried to make her tougher. They wanted to shield her, in an attempt to protect her from the world. However, the heart wants what the heart wants. So, Laura evolved her personality exactly the way she was supposed to, even though she was fed up with all the criticism she had received all these years.

When she finished her studies, she was meant to start working at the family business. Laura had other plans, though. Her dreams included helping others, and she pursued her volunteer work. The family did not share her enthusiasm, so there were constant fights about what she would do in her life. This whole situation had taken its toll on Laura, who felt trapped in something she could not escape. Emotionally, she was unable to express what she wanted. After a while, this led to a feeling of inadequacy, as she believed she did not have the power to be heard.

From the first moment I met Laura, I could tell she was an extraordinary woman. Her passion was evident, and it was really discomforting to see that she felt unhappy in her own close environment. The spark in her eyes was there, however. So, it was a pleasure to have endless conversations with Laura as to how she would like her life to be. We started Reiki sessions, and she found great comfort in restoring her inner balance. She felt in sync with the energy of the world, and she was looking forward to putting that into practice.

Just a couple of sessions were enough for her to understand her calling. She would pass on that knowledge to others, trying to relieve them of their pain. What can be more noble than that? Laura spread the word of Reiki, and she made sure that many people would know about it. As a result, she attuned quite a few. Her happiness was genuine, as she saw others smiling with joy, rather than feeling agony.

What I love most about Laura is her unquenched thirst for creation. She has always gone above and beyond toward helping others in a productive way. As a Reiki practitioner, Laura is now able to assist more people in reaching their inner level of spirituality. She continues on her path, and she is happier than ever. It is indeed moving to see how blissful someone feels through solidarity and mutual assistance.

Jason B.

One more story that I would like to share with you is that of Jason. He is a gifted man, filled with joy. He is an optimist, and some would say that he is a hopeless romantic. Unfortunately, life was not always kind to Jason. He had to go through a rough time, growing up without a family. As a consequence, he was forced to experience the injustice of life early on in his life. This obviously affected him deeply, even if he did not want to admit that. He was convinced that he would have to toughen up and conceal his true emotions.

As he grew up, he couldn't help but notice the emotional turmoil he found himself in, and he tried to come up with a solution. He has grown up believing that he would need to be independent, without requiring anyone to come and rescue him. So, he experimented with various different approaches to healing his wounded soul. Eventually, he came across Reiki. Just like many people, Jason was hesitant to trust something so out of his comfort zone. Nevertheless, he did. He gave it a shot, after talking to me extensively about what was troubling his mind.

We started the sessions, and I felt the tension and sadness all around his body. Slowly but steadily, we managed to overcome these difficulties. The first results came pretty soon. They only made Jason try harder. He pulled through, and eventually he thrived. This was all on him. He tried so hard, and now he enjoys the fruit of his hard labor. To my surprise, as soon as he found inner peace, he immediately wanted to know how he could help others manifesting the same problems. He became a Reiki healer, and he now has his own Reiki clinic.

I am so proud of people like Jason. They have come so far, based on their own power of will. Jason had suffered in his life. Yet, he did not give up. In fact, he accomplished what he had set his mind on. More than that, he devoted his life to helping more people in that situation. He contributes to the improvement of people's lives, with a practical solution to their problems. By doing so, he feels complete. An amazing feeling!

CHAPTER 7
CREATE A POWERFUL ROUTINE

Consistency is a crucial part of your Reiki experience, and it pretty much determines whether your efforts will bear fruit. It does not make sense to sporadically indulge in such a holistic treatment, expecting to get the full array of wonderful outcomes. You ought to devote some time to study, as well as practice what you have learned throughout your readings. This is the way to obtain mental clarity, as well as spiritual awareness and a deep connection with the universe.

In order to stick to your regimen, you must make sure that it is viable. Most people tend to be overly enthusiastic with their new beginnings. After a few days, they realize that they have set the bar too high. Instead of adjusting the regimen to their individual needs, they end up giving up altogether. So, all the efforts, all the plans, all the hopes for something great, go to waste. You should be proactive and think ahead. Otherwise, a plan that is impossible to adhere to in the long run will not offer you much.

Therefore, it is important to take into account your own individualized needs, your lifestyle, and your preferences. For instance, there is no point in incorporating a daily jog for a whole hour, even though you have never jogged in your life. It doesn't matter if you want to work out; the chances are that you will fail to stick to this routine. Instead, you should ease your way into this plan of yours, intensifying it as you go. When you feel comfortable with the first baby steps, then you can try to tighten your belt an extra notch.

Humans are creatures of habit. This means that we form behavioral patterns, which stay with us for a long time— sometimes for a lifetime. If you want to change your routine, then you need to do it methodically. Start slow and change even more when you feel good about the habit that you have just formed. In this way, you will be sure you can handle the change. You will not be put off or overwhelmed by the intensity of these modifications in your life. On the contrary, you will welcome them; after all, you will notice the results, which are going to motivate you even further.

A powerful Reiki routine will help you achieve your goals, in a positive manner. First, you must clarify your intentions. What are you trying to achieve through your routine? Are you mainly interested in relieving your pain, or are you intrigued by the opportunity to reach the highest levels of spiritual clarity? Do you want to address a chronic health condition, or do you mostly want to focus on your well-being? Is your main goal to change your life, attract wealth, or get rid of toxic relationships? As soon as you have answered these questions, you are ready to form your strategy.

By now, you have acquired the knowledge to put theory into practice. Nevertheless, you should be sure that you know what you are doing. Misconceptions often lead to negative effects, which in turn have an impact on the fundamental concept of Reiki. In order for you to practice Reiki, alone or with the contribution of a seasoned Reiki healer, you need to know what to expect. Otherwise, you are walking in the middle of a highway blindfolded, and your only hope is that the drivers all see you in time. Why take the risk of jeopardizing your well-being? You are responsible for your own actions, so be sure to learn everything in advance.

It is crucial to handle the energy properly. Reiki is all about energy, after all. If you do not know how to manage and preserve energy, then you are in trouble. Obviously, there are energy centers within your body. This is where the energy flows through, and this is where you should focus, in case of energy blocks. However, there are times when the energy feels overpowering. Unless you know how to channel it, you will end up being drained of your own personal energy, without any way of recovering. To that end, you should start slow, and make sure that you are up to the challenge.

Some Reiki healers claim that the healing process can have that effect on your physical body. As a consequence, you need to be aware of a potential energy drop during the first Reiki sessions. If you feel all right, you can proceed with caution. On the contrary, if you think that the energy drops messes with your well-being and prevents you from functioning like you should, then you need to postpone the session. Get some rest, because this is of paramount importance in Reiki. When you have fully recovered your strength, give it another go.

One of the basic things for you to consider is creating a sanctuary. This is going to be your sacred place, the one place in the world where you feel safe. In this sanctuary, you are going to spend your efforts toward balancing your inner energy. You will relax, let go of your worries, dispose of toxicity, and reach out to your dreams. Unless you have a place where you feel free, you cannot start this transformation in your life. So, be sure to create a welcoming place, where everything feels like home. It doesn't have to be anything fancy; it just needs to "speak" to you.

How to Form the Perfect Setting

Reiki is meant to take you on a spiritual journey, where you find yourself and your unique energy. You will be in absolute alignment with your surroundings, feeling the universal flow of energy in sync with yours. This is a wonderful and life-changing experience. A whole new world of potentials unveils before you. In order to wholeheartedly immerse in this experience, you need the proper setting. Everything around you should awaken your senses, stimulating you to let go of anything that has been holding you down.

Most people create a peaceful setting in order to practice Reiki. This is the ideal place to be, as it allows you to clear your mind and focus on what you are experiencing. Absolute serenity is beneficial to your soul and your emotional clarity. It enables you to reach your inner self and connect with the world without any distractions. Hence, a tranquil setting always acts positively in Reiki. That being said, though, you can literally practice Reiki anywhere. You can do it outdoors, by the beach, at a park, or even at your family apartment, in the garden, or out on the terrace.

There are no actual guidelines as to how this place needs to be. You are free to decorate it any way you feel like, adding things that make you smile. However, this doesn't mean that all places are equally inspirational. For example, you must pay attention to the light. You are inviting the light in, aren't you? How can you do that in a dark room? Sunlight should flow in the room, bathing the premises and creating an idyllic scenery. At the same time, you need to concentrate on the atmosphere. It should be bright but also airy. Large windows, perhaps light curtains, and adequate ventilation will do the trick.

Another thing you need to consider is the architecture, as well as the design of the interior spaces. As a rule of thumb, you do not want anything too stuffed, or you will feel as if the room is suffocating you. Instead, you must have enough space to perform your rituals. This will allow you to expand, without feeling restrained in any way. Moreover, you need to consider the furniture. Whatever you do, make sure you leave enough room. There is no need to add too many things within a small room, as it is going to have the opposite effect of what you want to achieve.

Lanterns and light fixtures hanging from the ceiling, as

well as bedside lamps and even smaller spotlights, will illuminate your room. You need as much light as you can get. Nonetheless, you must be careful when you choose the type of light. Warm light is more relaxing, whereas cool light is sharper. If you go for cool light, you will end up feeling exhausted after a while. This is not the best tip, if you want to soothe your senses. The same goes for colored light. It is best to avoid it, although at some point warm colors can have a positive effect on your mood. Candlelight is always a magnificent way to optimize your relaxation journey, though.

Music is up to you. If you like, you can have some soft, inspirational music playing in the background. It needs to be subtle, though. Nothing too loud because it will mess with the entire healing experience. When you are in pursuit of relaxation, you need the most suitable soundtrack. Lounge music, Zen, instrumental songs, sounds of East Asia, or even waves—these are all amazing options that will accompany you throughout your journey. It is equally important, though, to ensure you keep your room tidy and uncluttered. A messy place does not promote the sensation of absolute tranquility, in perfect harmony with the universe.

Many people choose to burn sage. This is a refreshing scent, clearing the air and getting rid of toxicity. If you are looking for a way to dispose of negative thoughts, sage might help. It enables your spirit to travel far away, as well as relaxes your mind and soothes your soul. Some others prefer scented candles. The lovely aromas of cinnamon, lavender, citrus, rose petals, or even chocolate will definitely create a cozy ambiance. Sandalwood is amazing, too. As a result, you will feel comfortable, at ease, and ready to wander through those mystical pathways you have set out to discover. Alternatively, you can use scented sticks, essential oils, or even aromatherapy sets. Whatever works best for you.

It would be great to invest in a Reiki table. This is the perfect tool which will allow you to relax. You need something soft, yet not too much. The mattress must be of high quality and ideally hypoallergenic. There are foldable Reiki beds out there, in case you do not have enough space in the room. Nevertheless, you can also choose to use any mattress, bed, or sofa. Just make sure that it does not bother you when you lie on it. Soft cushions are always welcome, as they add to the comforting atmosphere and assist you in feeling even more relaxed. Furthermore, you can add them when you experience even the slightest discomfort.

The chromatic palette in your sanctuary is completely your own decision. You are welcome to experiment with different colors or textures. In general, you should keep in mind that you need the room to be grounded with the environment. This means that you ought to select earthy tones for the colors of the walls, the furniture, and the fabrics. Wood is a great material to use throughout the room, from the floor to the furniture and the décor. However, there is enough room for mixing and blending. My personal preference is to choose brown, beige, and certainly white tones. Still, you can add your personal taste through colorful details. A pillow, a decorative candle, colorful bowls, and small rugs can make a huge difference.

Other things to review for your Reiki sanctuary include a yoga mat, a couple of inspirational posters, and possibly some plants. Orchids are exceptional, while you can also find dragon trees, Chinese evergreen, or philodendron. These are just a few of the best houseplants that require minimal care, so they can survive and make your room feel homey. A meditation blanket is another great addition, as it will enable you to define your own, personal space. Healing crystals can decorate the room, besides taking part in the Reiki healing process. In addition, you can buy a Tibetan bowl. It is beautiful, and it also creates vibrations meant to awaken different chakras. Of course, you are free to buy anything else that makes you happy and promotes your connection to divine energy.

Practical Tips

Reiki should be seen as a holistic experience. It does not only target your mind or your body. On the contrary, it is a mild, subtle way to promote healing on different levels. By now, you know how to use Reiki to clear the negative energy and enhance your body's healing powers. However, practicing Reiki is not all it takes for you to enjoy the vast benefits stemming from your connection with the world. This journey has a lot to offer, but you need to open up to a whole new mentality. There are things you need to modify if you are determined to go all the way, aiming at the absolute Reiki experience.

By adopting Reiki, you have made the first step toward a healthier, happier lifestyle. Is it enough? Some would say that you have done enough. You have acknowledged the existence of a universal life force, and you want to be part of it. Yet, you can do so much more than that. Reiki is your driving force, so as to enjoy every moment. When you make a decision to change, do not hold back. Instead, find everything that has kept you from your goals, and reverse the situation. It is in your hands now.

A simple, yet crucial decision is to start eating healthy, wholesome food. I know that the market features a cornucopia of goods, so it is almost impossible to decide what to consume. There are products covering different tastes and preferences. Nonetheless, just a fraction of these products is good for you, nutrition wise. Rather than buying overly processed food, packed with artificial substances and chemicals, you should opt for seasonal fruits, vegetables, and food with as little processing as possible. This will help you remain healthy, avoiding those food toxins that will poison you from within. At the same time, it is important to hydrate your body properly. By drinking plenty of water, you benefit your every cell, while removing the excess toxins from your body. This is particularly important, after having finished your Reiki session.

Sleep is an essential part of your life, whether you like it or not. There are people who believe that sleeping is a waste of time. This could not be further from the truth. In fact, during sleep your body regains a valuable amount of energy. Throughout the day, it goes without saying that the body becomes depleted of energy, hence it needs to recharge—just like a battery. More than that, sleep gives the opportunity to all the body organs to abstain from hard work. In this way, these body organs fuel up for another day filled with challenges. Detoxification takes place when you sleep, which makes absolute sense. At the same time, growth hormones are activated at night. So, in any event, sleep is an indispensable part of your life. You cannot live without it, nor should you want to do so.

Without sleep, you cannot get quality rest. This is particularly important for Reiki. Unless you gain the right balance between your body, your mind, and your soul, your energy flow will never be ideal. As a result, your performance at Reiki will not be what you have been hoping to achieve. Some people might not realize that, but this is in fact one of the biggest downfalls when you practice Reiki. It doesn't matter if you want to complete the session. If your body is so tired that it does not cooperate, then there is nothing more that you can do.

To avoid that energy drainage that poses a great hindrance to your progress, you ought to be very meticulous when it comes to sleep patterns. Be sure to get enough sleep to make it through the day. Eight hours of quality sleep may sound too much, but it is absolutely necessary for your body to reboot. You also need to make sure that you rest right before your session. This means that you should avoid any intense workouts at least an hour before your Reiki session. The same goes for the time period after practicing Reiki. Allow your body some time to recover.

If you truly want to experience the greatness of Reiki, you should connect with nature. During the session, you feel the overpowering energy passed on to you by the Reiki healer. Still, this is not enough. You must take advantage of every opportunity you get, in order to explore nature's magnitude. Go out for a walk at the park, arrange for an excursion, take a leisurely stroll by the beach. Listen to the waves or the gentle breeze touching the trees. Smell the rose gardens and the herbs on the patios. Enjoy watching a marvelous sunrise or a sunset. These are all moments when you can connect with nature, getting even closer. These are moments to cherish.

Before starting your Reiki session and after wrapping up this spiritual experience of yours, it is vital that you indulge in stretching. By stretching, you prepare your body for what is about to take place. You enhance its flexibility, so as to maintain its power and allow you to fully relax. Your body is like a shrine, and you need to treat it as such. Rather than beginning your Reiki session abruptly, you can stretch your neck, your arms, and legs. In this manner, you can expect a deeper sense of relaxation. Your exercises will not put strain on your body, and you will recover more efficiently. Upon finishing the Reiki healing session, stretching will enable your body to avoid any injury.

Your neck experiences most of the tension, so it makes perfect sense that you start with a set of basic neck stretches. First of all, you should stand upright. Put your left arm behind your back, right where the spine begins. Now, tilt your head toward your right shoulder, and put your right hand on the left side of your neck. In this way, you will be able to push a little further during your stretch. Rest there for around 30 seconds and repeat the other way around. Another neck stretch includes the very same opening position, standing upright. In this stretch, you do not tilt your head. You turn it a little, so that you reach for your shoulder. Last but not least, you can put both your hands on either side of your head, elbows bent. Push your head forward, until your chin touches your chest. Rest there for around 30 seconds and return to your starting position.

Apart from stretching, you can also incorporate therapeutic massage into your daily routine. There are differences between Reiki and massage treatments, of course. However, they both target relaxation, as well as healing specific diseases through a more natural perspective. Depending on your specific needs, you can request a massage of your upper body, a massage of your limbs, or even a scalp massage. Whatever you do, you will feel immensely more relaxed afterward. Even if you are sensitive to touch, you can start slow and test your tolerance. Massage treatments can be sporadic or more frequent according to what you like. Give it a chance, and you will be amazed at the sensation you get.

Emotional Freedom Technique (EFT), otherwise known as Tapping, can be used in combination with Reiki for exceptional results (Tapping/EFT, n.d.). If I had to compare EFT with another holistic treatment, this would definitely be acupuncture. They both believe that any negative experience comes from the imbalance of energy within the body.

Moreover, they both base their treatment on the meridian points within the body. There are 12 different meridian points in the body, each of which reflects a different body organ. Acupuncture has needles to restore that imbalance.

On the other hand, EFT does not penetrate the skin. In that sense, it is far less invasive than acupuncture. Still, it targets the very same spots on the body, and it does so through tapping. It is impressive to see how tapping can have a direct effect on the way your body works, in sync with the mind and the spirit. EFT practitioners adjust the intensity of the tap depending on the severity of the issue at hand. If the problem is light, then tapping is gentle. On the contrary, a grave abnormality calls for more powerful tapping. In any case, the end result aims at stimulating the energy centers to flow more smoothly.

As you can see, the full Reiki experience penetrates every single aspect of your lifestyle. By introducing you to a whole new world of opportunities to relax and restore your inner balance, it offers you great healing benefits and lifts your spirit. This is an integrated experience, meant to treasure your individuality, while simultaneously celebrating your connection with the entire universe. Don't think about it—dive right in!

CHAPTER 8
USE REIKI TO HEAK YOURSELF
AND OTHERS

R eiki is a powerful tool, which can be used to transform your life. It can also be used as a means to help others turn their life around, through the healing power it offers. Wouldn't you like to help yourself and others? There is nothing more noble than passing on your knowledge, in order to improve someone else's life. This is one of the best things about Reiki, as it focuses not only on your own prosperity and health. It also teaches you to be humble and help others any way you can.

There are distinctive levels of Reiki knowledge, passed on from a Reiki master to the students. According to your own intent, you can either choose to stay at the first degree or aim at the highest level of Reiki mastery. First of all, you need to keep in mind the fact that there are different requirements for each degree of attunement. No one claims that being a Reiki master is ideal for everybody. On the contrary, there are people who are better off as students.

If you are interested in the first degree of Reiki (or else known as Shoden), then you can receive that either in one session or in a set of four different courses. It depends on the Reiki master you turn to. In any case, this is the lowest level of Reiki understanding. The student opens up to this whole new world of opportunities, where the energy centers receive the universal energy force. The attunement involves the energy flow straight from the top of the head to the heart, and finally the hands. As you can imagine, no one can expect to experience Reiki without reaching the first degree.

The second degree of Reiki is called Okuden. There are two features in this option, including the practice of Reiki to others and the deeper connection of energy flow for yourself. So, if someone is eager to dive into the mysteries of Reiki and pass on their knowledge to other people, then the second level of

Reiki is a great place to start. Typically, a three months' period is required before receiving your second attunement. However, this can vary. If you lead a busy lifestyle, then you will need a wider time period prior to moving on to the next step.

Finally, there is the level of being a Reiki master. This degree is also called Shinpiden, and not all Reiki students reach that, even if they set out to do so. When you receive the final attunement, you are able to teach others. However, not everyone feels good about teaching. This is why some people receive the level of Reiki master but still do not practice what they have learned on other individuals. In order to complete that master attunement, you must first cover the basics. So, it makes perfect sense that you need to follow the right order, starting at the bottom and reaching the top. The entire procedure takes up to a year to complete, but you can adjust it at your own pace.

If you are wondering why you need to get a license to practice Reiki with others, then think of it exactly like any other profession. Licensed professionals prove that they are capable of doing the work that they have been claiming to offer. They have been tested and found adequate to live up to the challenges. This means that you can expect a minimum level of quality in the services provided, which brings peace of mind to many people. Would you ever trust a dentist who had no diploma from a university? Would you even trust a store lacking the proper license to operate? There really is no argument in that.

Another issue to keep in mind is that the nature of a Reiki practitioner is pretty fluid, which means that everybody can claim to be one. Does this mean that it is that easy to become a master in Reiki energy? Not at all. It basically means that you should be suspicious and not trust anyone telling you that they are experts. Either trust somebody recommended to you by a common friend or choose a qualified, licensed professional to help you out on your journey. In many ways, that person is going to be a mentor for you. Do not take that decision lightly, as it is going to determine the course of your own progress.

If you want to open a Reiki clinic, always make sure that you comply with the local legislation in the place where you wish to operate. Find a cozy place to create your personal sanctuary and use your connections. It would be prudent to search at the local clubs and the organizations of Reiki, so as to find some useful insight on your competition. At the same time, you will have the opportunity to benefit from the wisdom of those who have already set up their business before you. They will know what to look out for and what to avoid like the plague. It goes without even questioning, though, that you will be required to offer your own seasoned look in the future, in the spirit of solidarity.

Are you drawn by the opportunity to heal others and maybe even pass on your knowledge and wisdom deriving from personal experience? Then, you should consider becoming a Reiki master. It will give you great joy to watch others, as they basically unveil the abundant light of the universe. It is that sense of discovering the very fabric of the world, depicted through the raw force of energy. The universe is purely mesmeric, and it is a privilege to understand even the slightest bits and pieces. Once you fully comprehend what it means to make use of Reiki power to change your life, it is like you have just found a chest filled with golden coins, precious gems, and invaluable possessions. There is so much to do with that.

Reiki is all about personal connection. It is the feeling of connecting with the world around you on a deeper level of understanding. There is nothing more uplifting than this, knowing you can defy the barriers put before you, so as to become part of something greater. Reiki teaches you selflessness and to be an unconditional help to those in need. It teaches you how to be grateful for everything that you have received in your life, as well as humble for your accomplishments. There is no room for ego boosts here, as Reiki focuses on the balance of the universe in unity. No one stands alone in this.

That very philosophy has attracted attention from people of different backgrounds, who have sought after the opportunity to expand their horizons and become part of Reiki. If you feel like this description suits you, then you should consider climbing up the ladder and becoming a Reiki master yourself. In this way, you will be capable of teaching others and helping them get in that sacred passage of deeper life understanding.

Moving forward, I am going to analyze two different aspects of Reiki. First of all, self-treatment Reiki is used all over the world, and it enables the students to take charge of their healing process. Isn't that wonderful? The second aspect of Reiki is that of distant healing. In a world where distance might be daunting, it is comforting to know that there is another way. There is a way to eliminate distance and connect even from afar. It might seem impossible, but the truth will prove you wrong.

Reiki Self-Treatment

You have the option of healing yourself through Reiki. Even if you do not want to schedule a Reiki session and receive the universal energy force from the Reiki practitioner, you can still handle everything on your own. Through Reiki self-treatment sessions, you are free to benefit from the magnificent features of Reiki, without anyone else having to be present. In fact, once you become accustomed to the process, you will realize that it is actually easier to do that.

Many people choose Reiki self-treatment due to its flexibility and ease of use. You do not have to coordinate with someone else, trying to figure out when and where to proceed. Furthermore, you can fit the healing treatment to your own schedule, depending entirely on the way you feel and the things that you have to do. If you like, you can divide the healing process into two different sessions. In this way, you can start early in the morning and continue later in the evening, as soon as you have wrapped up your busy day.

If you want to try it out, you need to follow a strategy that works well for you. In other words, you must feel comfortable and pleasant while performing Reiki on your own. Otherwise, it will not be long until you give up and fall into the same patterns again. Obviously, you need to adhere to the same guidelines that apply to Reiki sessions with another individual. For example, you should find a peaceful sanctuary, so as to be able to relax. Ideally, you need to be alone when performing your Reiki self-treatment. Wear light clothes, which allow your body to breathe; make sure that the temperature in the room is neither hot nor cold.

Once you have created a welcoming atmosphere, with the soft music and the inspiring scents that help you travel within your mind, indulge yourself in a session of no less than 20 minutes. It is important that you make the time, so as to reap the benefits you are entitled to from the entire procedure. As to the exercises of the self-treatment session, there is no actual plan to be followed by all Reiki practitioners. Below, I am going to describe some of the most frequently used positions in Reiki for self-healing sessions.

You should start by placing your palms touching each other, right in front of your chest. Your elbows need to be bent, and you ought to focus on your breathing. Keep your eyes closed and become aware of your surroundings. Enjoy the echoing sound of silence, as it floods the room. Then, you can place your hands on top of your head. In this way, you touch your Crown Chakra, and you become more connected to your spirituality. This will allow you to become more conscious and concentrate.

When you are in this position with your hands on top of your head, you can try to lift the skin from your forehead, moving upward. As you do that, you get to relax the muscles on your head. That alone makes you feel better at once. Now cover your eyes with your palms. Another great position, which helps you relax even more. For your balance, you can place your hands on either side of your head, covering your ears.

By using gentle movements, you can then place your hands over your shoulders. It will feel like you are trying to embrace yourself. Your right palm will be placed on top of your left shoulder, and your left palm will then be placed on your right shoulder, creating a virtual hug. This is an excellent position, promoting acceptance. In a similar pattern, you can then place your hands over your throat. This is where your Throat Chakra is located, after all. So, this position enables communication.

It is time to move toward the heart. Place both your palms on top of your chest, right where the heart is located. Compassion and love are the two main elements in this particular area. If you experience emotional discomfort, then you need to prolong this position. Breathe deeply, inhale, and exhale. Let your mind get rid of all the negativity that has been piling up there. When you feel confident, move your hands in front of your solar plexus. This represents your personal power. Push your hands a little, as if you are trying to touch your spine through the solar plexus. Then, move them to your abdomen. The upper abdomen has to do with issues in digestion. If you are troubled by that, then feel free to prolong this position.

Afterward, move to the lower abdomen. There, you deal with your emotions. In addition, this is the part where your most intimate desires nestle. If you are having trouble with your reproductive system or if you are going through a rough time with your sexual partner, then you need to concentrate on this position for a while.

This concludes the basic position at the front of your body. Next, you can place your hands in the back, exactly where your spine starts. As a result, you will promote grounding. You know how essential this can be for your attempt to connect with the world.

Before you finish your Reiki self-treatment ritual, you can place your hands in front of your thighs, then the knees, and finally your feet. It is best to start from the top of your head, at the Crown Chakra, and move all the way down to the ground. This is the normal course of energy flow. It starts high above your own body and finishes where your feet touch the ground, representing your connection with the spiritual, alongside the physical world.

Drink a glass of water or a cup of warm, herbal tea. It will soothe your senses and allow you to maintain your calmness for a long time. Stretch a little, and then be sure to contemplate what you have experienced throughout your Reiki session. Are you content with the results? Or do you feel like you could do more? Either way, it is good to experiment and use your hands to wander through the parts of your body, where you have the most tension. If you notice that there are energy blocks in your joints or in front of your chest, then you should target those parts. It is crucial to release the tension and restore the smooth energy flow to balance your body.

It is safe to assume that self-care is much more than a couple of Reiki sessions within the day. On the contrary, it depicts your attitude toward your most precious belonging. In order for you to succeed in your spiritual goals, you first need to prove that you love yourself, deeply and unconditionally. You love yourself, no matter what has happened along the way. There are no asterisks, no small print that can change the way you feel. After all, the most important thing in life is to recover from all the negative things that have come your way, making room for the exceptional things about to happen.

Your journey is a long one, as it covers your entire life, since birth. It makes sense that not everything has turned out the way you anticipated. Problematic behaviors, toxic relationships, hardships that no one can avoid, difficulties on a number of different levels (mental, emotional, physical)—all these elements have created an explosive environment. If you wait too long, you risk an explosion of unprecedented severity, which is going to affect every inch of your body, your mind, and your soul.

To avoid such a dramatic explosion, you need to take measures. It is in your hands to reverse the situation, helping yourself to recover. Unless you come to terms with your presence in the world, you cannot make any real improvement. First and foremost, you ought to discover who you are. Then, you ought to reassess your priorities and start thinking about who you want to be. Once you have found the right balance, you will be able to claim the change you have always hoped to experience.

No matter how many times you have failed, it is your duty to try once more. If you are determined to succeed, it will happen eventually. But by beating yourself up and feeling guilt over every single thing that you do, you leave no room for improvement. You are caught up in a vortex, and you allow it to drain you of your energy. Do not let that happen. Put your feet on the ground and set your goals. Make feasible changes, which can take place gradually, rather than all at once. In this way, you will have the chance to track your progress as you go.

Remember that it is a marathon, not a sprint. Your aim is to make it to the finish line. No one cares about the world record. What you should focus on is your personal evolution and your achievements throughout this entire experience. You are setting the course, so it is up to you to determine where you are headed.

Distance Reiki Healing

On a slightly different note, there is a distance Reiki healing option for you to consider. If for whatever reason you cannot physically be close to your Reiki master, then you can try this out and see if it ticks all the boxes for you. In fact, it might come as a pleasant surprise to realize just how powerful Reiki can be. After all, Reiki does not depend on touching. Some Reiki healers do not even touch the students during the session. They either place their hands right above the body parts that they wish to focus on, or they just visualize the entire attunement process.

There is a growing need to pass on Reiki energy flow to people all over the world. Many people cannot afford visiting a Reiki clinic or cannot even move. Moreover, there are people who do not feel comfortable putting their trust in others face to face; they are more prone to do that with physical barriers in place. This means that a slightly hesitant individual will not feel good about trusting a complete stranger. On the other hand, the very same individual will most likely have no problem whatsoever trying out a treatment online.

Another benefit you get from distance Reiki healing is the fact that you can do it anywhere you feel like it. For example, you can schedule a distant Reiki healing session while you are at home, on vacation, even at the office. Of course, you need at least some private space. Otherwise, chances are that someone, or something, is going to mess with your concentration. You need to maintain your serenity, so this is the only requirement you should adhere to if you decide to experiment with distant healing.

Before the session, you need to make the necessary arrangements with the Reiki healer. In this way, you will know what to expect. There is nothing worse than someone catching you unprepared. Hence, you should ask any questions you might have. Is there anything troubling you? Do you have any comments as to the entire Reiki session? Ask away, and the Reiki healer will be more than happy to provide you with answers. It is important that you enter into the Reiki course, without anything on your mind. Nothing should worry you or stand in the way between yourself and the healing process.

Even though you will be far away from the Reiki healer, it is essential that you lie down. You won't get the results you are entitled to unless you commit to the session. Reiki healers do their part, even from a distance; it is up to you to receive the energy coming your way. In order to do that, you must open up to the healing treatment after it has begun. Therefore, you must be careful not to distract yourself in any way during the

Reiki session. Otherwise, you are risking losing invaluable energy and compromising the benefits you do receive in the end. Why would you ever want to sabotage your efforts like that?

You can either choose to do it over the phone or online. In that case, you can connect to Skype or any other messaging application and proceed with the session. Some Reiki practitioners, however, offer the option of completely distant sessions. They use the technique of visualization in order to achieve that. Long distance is not an issue for them. They have mastered specific attunements to be used under such conditions. To help them out, these healers might use special healing symbols, as well as accessories throughout the Reiki course.

Listen to the special instructions that your Reiki healer provides prior to your session. You will most probably be expected to drink plenty of water, and special mention should be given to your sleep patterns. In order for the energy flow to run smoothly, you will need to be perfectly restful. If you are already exhausted, your energy drainage will take its toll on your performance. You will not have the chance to receive the blessings that your Reiki practitioner sends your way, diminishing the aftereffects of your healing.

One of the biggest drawbacks in distance Reiki healing is the fact that the Reiki students find it hard to concentrate. When you lack the personal touch, it is difficult to realize exactly what happens during the session. Sure, the feeling that you get is often so intense that it overpowers any doubt. However, the truth is that nothing can replace personal connection. From afar, every party seems to be consumed by their own agenda. At the clinic, both the healer and the student share a common ground. They will be in the same room, interacting with each other. In this case, the conditions are quite different.

If I had to compare it to an experience, this would definitely be like sharing an important, heartfelt conversation over the phone. Even if the intentions are good, the quality of the phone connection can never match that of face-to-face communication. In the former, the means limit you in a way. The latter allows you immense freedom. You can touch the person next to you, comfort them through the slightest gestures that prove you are empathizing with them. A nod, a look, a smile—these are all subtle yet so powerful when connecting to others. In Reiki, the healer connects deeply with the student. Physical presence is not necessary, but it certainly adds to the overall experience.

In a nutshell, distance Reiki healing is an alternative treatment for those who cannot, or will not, schedule a Reiki session in person. It can act as a great way of eliminating space and time. There are great benefits stemming from such an option. However, it cannot fully replace the real physical presence and the connection achieved through the interaction of the Reiki healer and the student. It would be best if you combined distant healing along with face-to-face Reiki sessions, in order to receive the optimal effects.

CONCLUSION

By now, I am sure that you know what it means to practice Reiki. You have read through its origins, as well as its fundamental principles. You know what it feels like to connect to the world around you, finding the perfect balance with nature. More than that, you know that it works. You have seen it from your own experience and through careful observation. The stories that I have shared with you hopefully inspired you to dive into the magical world of spirituality, in pursuit of a healthier, happier lifestyle.

In the different chapters of this book, I have tried to explain the powerful energy flow through our body's chakras. I have laid out the different meanings of healing crystals, symbols used in Reiki, and various approaches. Reiki is used to fight disease, as a complementary form of treatment that is both subtle and extremely effective. It allows you to open up to a whole new world, where spirituality is celebrated through the right balance of your inner self. You find mental clarity, emotional peace, and alignment with the physical world.

Once you set out on this wonderful journey of a lifetime, you will realize this is how your life should have been in the first place. Nowadays, even in the most hectic moments of our life, we do feel like we need to slow down. We need to return to our roots, identifying what has been poisoning our very existence. There is no other way. One of the biggest problems of modern society is that we have run out of time. We are so anxious to make things happen that we tend to forget what actually matters. The consequences of such a frenzied daily routine are tremendous, and people are now more stressed than ever before.

This is where Reiki steps in. Whether you want to become a Reiki healer or simply follow the philosophy of this noninvasive healing process, you will feel a great relief. There are many people who have tried Reiki in their life and have found an excellent way to channel their energy, improving different aspects of their daily routine. Depending on the issues that have been troubling them, Reiki can unblock the energy abnormalities found in one's body, restoring balance and enabling a breath of fresh air. I am not trying to make things complicated.

Reiki dates back to ancient times, where the power of the universe was praised, and people followed a natural course in life. The teachings of the past can reflect in today's world, introducing us to a whole new perspective. Rather than worrying about too much, we can focus on the present and let the healing properties of the universal energy force surround us. What can be better than the return to a tranquil, balanced way of life?

Besides the theoretical background of Reiki, this book provides you with hands-on advice on how to start incorporating Reiki into your lifestyle. It inspires you to create the perfect peaceful setting, with special practical tips and the addition of wonderful accessories that enhance your Reiki experience. Moreover, it offers you guidance as to how to become a Reiki master and practice what you have been taught to pass on your knowledge to others. Learn more about the attunements or initiations required to reach the different levels of Reiki mastery.

In this book, I also introduced you to a method used to overcome boundaries of space and time. You saw how you can even practice distance Reiki healing, so as to offer the benefits of universal energy force regardless of physical limitations. Does this sound intriguing to you? You also learned how to unblock your chakras and clear negative energy from around you. Attract positive outcomes, through the power of your mind, your body, and your spirit. A splendid combination, which will transform your life from within.

I hope you enjoyed this book and that you found inspiration, as well as the wealth of information you need for healing yourself and others through Reiki. You have all the tools required to change what has been holding you back all this time. Reiki is much more than a philosophical trend, and it can improve your quality of life from day one. It is an exciting experience, and I am looking forward to welcoming you to a vivid Reiki community. Don't waste any more time, as time is invaluable. Indulge in the very essence of Reiki and enjoy your life like you should—you deserve it!

REFERENCES

Ancient Olympics. (n.d.). Ancientolympics.Arts.Kuleuven.Be. http://ancientolympics.arts.kuleuven.be/eng/TE010E N.html

Estrada, J. (2020, March 6). *5 reiki principles you can use to create more ease and flow in your life.* Well+Good. https://www.wellandgood.com/reiki-principles/

Hayes, A. (n.d.). *Reading into quid pro quo.* Investopedia. https://www.investopedia.com/terms/q/quidproquo. asp

Müller, A. (2020, June 3). *Kundalini energy: What it is and how to awaken it within you.* Medium. https://medium.com/mindfully-speaking/kundalini-energy-what-it-is-and-how-to-awaken-it-within-you-a542f8aa39ed

Rataic, T. (2016, March 7). *How to use reiki and the law of attraction to reach your goals - part 1.* The Reiki Guide. https://thereikiguide.com/how-to-use-reiki-and-the-law-of-attraction-to-reach-your-goals-part-1/

Schaedig, D. (2020, August 24). *Self-fulfilling prophecy and the Pygmalion effect.* Simply Psychology. https://www.simplypsychology.org/self-fulfilling-prophecy.html#:~:text=A%20self%2Dfulfilling%20pr ophecy%20is

Tantrik Studies. (2016, February 6). Hareesh.org. https://hareesh.org/blog/2016/2/5/the-real-story-on-the-chakras

Tapping/EFT. (n.d.). The Reiki Center. https://www.thereikicenter.net/tappingeft.html

The history of Usui reiki and the reiki principles | London |

Reiki training and meditation courses. (n.d.). Reiki-Meditation.Co.Uk.   ttps://www.reiki-meditation.co.uk/the-history-of-usui-reiki/

Wikipedia Contributors. (2019, February 21). *Placebo.* Wikipedia;   Wikimedia   Foundation. https://en.wikipedia.org/wiki/Placebo

Zoldan, R. J. (2020, June 22). *Your 7 chakras, explained plus how to tell if they're blocked.* Well+Good. https://www.wellandgood.com/what-are-chakras/

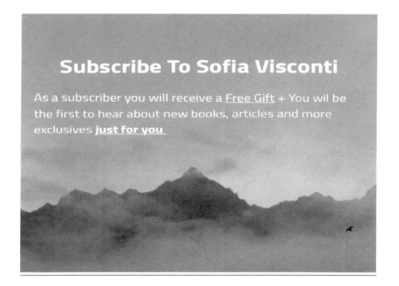

Click Here